WIN VIA TRUST

WIN

VIA

TRUST

The Practical Leadership Framework
to Build Trust, Close Deals, and
Deliver Exceptional Results

Michael Rabinowitz, MBA

ISBN (paperback): 979-8-9947277-0-6
ISBN (hardcover): 979-8-9947277-1-3
ISBN (ebook): 979-8-9947277-2-0
ISBN (audiobook): 979-8-9947277-3-7

Editorial services: Sandra Wendel, Write On, Inc.
Design: Marko Markovic, 5mediadesign

Published by Intelluvia Press, an imprint of Intelluvia LLC

Contact the author at
www.WinViaTrust.com and info@winviatrust.com

To my wife
and children

CONTENTS

INTRODUCTION

I T WAS AN IMPOSSIBLE SITUATION. WE had just one day to work with Cal Ripken Jr., the Hall of Fame shortstop for the Baltimore Orioles, to produce a year's worth of promotional literature, motivational short videos and clips, and still shots.

To give you some background, I was the product manager for a once-daily hypertension medicine, and with a tight promotional budget, my team needed to quickly create and reinforce a differentiated brand image that really stood out from the competitors, who would be spending three to four times the amount on their advertising. Cal Ripken Jr., besides being incredibly popular across our target audience, was in the midst of a record to play in 2,632 consecutive baseball games—a legendary "Iron Man" streak that will probably never be broken. There was no better way to reinforce a brand perception of working hard, each and every day, than through an association with Cal in the late 1980s.

Through agency outreach and efforts before I came into the role, we knew that he had sincere interest in healthcare and that he was willing to contract with us as long as we made clear that he did not have hypertension and used his image in a way that he was comfortable. The only downside was that we only had one day with him to film everything that we would need for thousands of promotional pieces throughout the year.

Of course, we did everything we could to prepare for that monumental day by getting all the promotional language and planned shots approved well ahead of time by Cal's agents and regulatory agencies as necessary. Still, I was experienced enough to know that expert planning and preparation might become only a footnote if there was poor execution.

I asked our advertising agency leader, Kevin, one last time, "Are you confident that we have everything we need?"

He said, "Don't worry at all, Michael, and just enjoy the day tomorrow."

We arrived early that morning at a large facility outside of Baltimore specifically equipped for video and photo productions. Our small team, together with our advertising agency, numbered fewer than ten people. Cal Ripken Jr. was right on time, what else would one expect, and his agent was quickly on the phone on other matters. It is not every day that you meet such a superstar, so I had prepared a thoughtful greeting. Before I could get out two words, Cal came over and just said, "It is a pleasure to meet you. Let's do it."

Our advertising agency gave him the uniform that he would wear for the filming, and after he changed, we walked through the day's plans. We began filming and everything went smoothly. Cal's agent checked in periodically to make sure that Cal was comfortable and reinforced to me that they would be leaving by 3:00, which was the plan. I continued to oversee everything, but really let the lighting, sound, and filming experts run with the plan.

When output was ready to be reviewed, Kevin would ask, "Looks great, doesn't it?" and I genuinely agreed. Only a few times I thought a photo should be retaken and everyone was happy to do so. It actually was becoming an enjoyable day.

With about ninety minutes left in our day with Cal, we moved to the part of the studio to take the action shot in which Cal would dive into some pillows to catch a baseball in his glove. Our advertising agency had consulted with colleagues who did this all the time to ensure the right equipment for maximizing this specific photo shoot and the safety of Cal. Kevin walked Cal through the set and what would happen, asking Cal, "Are you comfortable with everything?"

Cal responded, "Looks great."

Yet, as Cal was getting into position, his agent came over and said, "Wait a minute. I can't have Cal risking any injury. This won't work."

I completely understood the agent's point of view. How could Cal risk the all-time sports record for playing in consecutive games for the upside of doing a pharmaceutical photo shoot? The tradeoff made no sense, even if we were several months before the start of the season. However, the risk was way overblown, and we needed to quickly make him comfortable that there was essentially no risk.

While I had previously asked the question privately, I asked Kevin again so that the agent could hear the response, "Have we done everything possible to limit any risk of injury to Cal?"

"Yes," he said. "Let me catch the ball to show you what it looks like in action."

Kevin then proceeded to dive on the pillows and say, "See—unbelievably soft landing."

While it would have been even more impressive if he had caught the baseball, he made his point. Still, the agent was not fully on board. The ad agency's technical expert then spoke: "I talked to my friends at ESPN and this is how everybody does it." Then he added a few magic words. "Trust me. I am a lifelong baseball fan and would never put the greatest living legend at risk."

As well said as it was, the agent did not seem to buy it. Cal looked at the set and various machinery in greater detail, lifted one of the many pillows, and hit it with his open hand. He then said, "I trust you. Let's go."

Cal then jumped on the pillows to further test them out and communicated exactly where he would dive. He did a practice dive and gave a thumbs-up to everyone. That broke the silence in the studio, and you could hear people breathing again. Outside of further direction from Cal as to how high the ball should be thrown, the action shots went without a hitch. The photos proved to be the best of the day. The success on that day, which fueled the entire year's promotion, was all due to trust.

Through my experiences, working for over thirty years in large and small companies within executive and non-executive roles across various functions including marketing, sales, finance, information technology, and others, I led and learned from many initiatives and outcomes—both great successes and some failures.

One of my most challenging roles was to make business deals, either bring in new products (in-licensing or acquisition) or to move on from existing products (out-license or sale). In such roles, I rarely knew my counterparts at the other companies. I spent much of the time doing as much analysis as possible in terms of profiling different companies to uncover who might be willing to consider such opportunities, reaching out to them, and, then, if everything had gone well, I tried to maximize our company's returns by out negotiating the other party—not exactly the formula for building trust. Yet, ironically, if we could not establish trust, the deal would be dead.

Having a family and three children, I was also active in the community in coaching youth sports for decades and serving on boards of charities and in other voluntary roles. I quickly realized that the drivers of individual and group success were the same as in my professional work, just in different environments or reworded as different objectives. Trust was the critical ingredient that made people willing to work together or support the same cause. This is true for almost all collaborative efforts, even though the role of trust may not always be obvious.

This insight made it easy to focus on trust as a topic that I wanted to better explore for the purposes of sharing such learnings. Trust or being trustworthy, in their essence, allows people to go beyond themselves and collaborate. Since few endeavors can be done alone, trust opens up a world of possibilities. Trust is the glue that holds relationships together and permits societies to work collectively to achieve greatness. Despite its importance, many people treat trust as a disposable commodity, easily gained whenever needed and not worth the effort to maintain. If I could help people think about trust differently and place greater value and priority on becoming trustworthy, that would be a good day for them and—if I may be bold enough to venture—for all of us.

Not surprisingly, in a world of over 8 billion people, I am not the only one to think about writing a book about trust. The self-help section of a virtual or standing bookstore is filled with many books that state that they are the answer to all your trust questions. In addition, trust is so fundamental to relationships that some of the fiction classics are about trust at their core. Does anyone doubt the trust between Frodo and Sam in J.R.R. Tolkien's *The Lord of the Rings* or between Harry, Ron, and Hermione in J.K. Rowling's Harry Potter series?

This led me to conclude that the best way that I could add value to the conversation was to write this book from the unique vantage point of my varied experiences and insights, using a framework that constantly asks the question: Why does this matter and how should this change anything that I think or do? I believe that this unrelenting and focused lens of practicality could potentially deliver significantly more value to you, the reader, than other self-help books on trust.

Consistent with this approach, I have designed and will walk you through a 2x2 decision matrix as to whether a situation is trustworthy or not. I call it the Trustworthy Decision Matrix. Given that I have kept the Trustworthy Decision Matrix to two variables, the simplicity of the tool should make it easy to remember and execute. I apply this tool to various situations throughout the book to help you view its utility and application. Don't let its simplicity fool you to discount its utility.

I cover many aspects of trust but do not delve into the area of friendships and marriage as this is already well covered by the publishing community and would dilute the focus of the intended audience. I do address the religious aspects of trust because I acknowledge that, for many people, trust in G-d (a deep reverence and awe, grounded in Jewish law, strongly discourages writing the full name of the Divine, which is respected in this book) and the belief that there is divine purpose for each individual and the world can be the most powerful trust that guides a person's life and allows them to better cope with events that may be tragic or that they do not understand.

My goal is to provide meaningful context on the various aspects of trust, with each chapter starting with a relevant story from my experiences to offer more relatability. I then provide a review of existing studies, surveys, and evidence-based expertise to drive toward practical implications and conclusions. I rely on the experts and footnote their work. You can find the original citations in the extensive Notes section at the end.

Next, I summarize the wealth of data into one or two paragraphs for those who want a quick overview or review. In the section titled "The So What," I focus in more depth on how these trends and facts impact today's leader and suggest best practices to elevate your performance and growth.

I conclude each chapter with a few actionable steps to help make trust a key driver of success. To maintain the uniqueness of the book, all the material is presented within the lens of practicality and usability and leverages the Trustworthy Decision Matrix as relevant.

I trust that you have chosen this book to help you achieve a new level of leadership, and I aim to earn that trust. Let us begin.

1

THE TRUST ADVANTAGE

Y OU GOT TO GET DOWN HERE quick. This project is blowing up," a senior director in the business development department yelled. She was calling to tell me that the two companies that had been meeting for several weeks were now at an impasse.

"What can be so irreconcilable at this stage?" I asked her. "The opportunity is a classic win-win for both companies."

One company was a small, closely held European biotech that had recently developed a product that could be a game-changer for a devastating type of cancer. The product would need to undergo further clinical studies to confirm its safety and efficacy, which meant more cost and risk than the company could afford.

The other company was a global billion-dollar pharmaceutical corporation that I worked for and had the scale to perform such clinical trials along with the expertise and cost structure that minimized the risk. If the clinical studies were positive, there also was no better company to market the product than this large pharmaceutical company, which had always wanted to enter the cancer market without much success. It was a textbook case of an ideal match leading to a mutually transformative deal.

My colleague replied, "I don't think that our differences can be bridged." She was an expert at solving such problems, so I quickly understood the gravity of the situation. She continued, "It is not about money at all. Please come to our conference room, and I will explain more."

I put aside what I was working on and walked down to the conference room in another section of our main building. As I was walking, I was trying to think about different possibilities that could be blocking the progress. I had not been involved in this particular project but had been instrumental in several commercial negotiations led by this team. They were an excellent group, quite experienced at understanding the concerns of potential partners and addressing them through fair but tough negotiations.

I entered the private room that was filled with the negotiating team for the global pharma company. While no one could easily articulate the root cause to me, it seemed to center on the small company insisting on retaining the marketing rights to the product in France. "They want the product rights in France and won't budge," summarized another member of the negotiating team. Not surprisingly, the small company was based in France, which helped guide this perception.

From a bigger-picture view, it made little sense to either party financially to assign the rights in France to the small company, which had no sales force or other commercial capabilities. Yet sometimes ego or other reasons prevent a smaller company from making the rational decision to let their partner maximize the sales, especially in their home country. This typically is resolved by offering the holdout more money or providing them with an option to co-promote in that country, with the large company leading the commercialization decisions and operations.

I had not met with the small company previously, so after being briefed on their relevant background, I proposed, "Let me join the next meeting that you have with the smaller company to see if I can pick up on anything that may be helpful." It did not take long as the other company was in town for the entire week, and the next meeting was that afternoon.

After being introduced, I simply listened and observed. I could discern that the small company was generally quite engaged and forthcoming with information. Indeed, they were proud of their product. They seemed to respect the larger pharmaceutical company and were getting along well. You would not know that there was any issue at all.

During a break in the conversation, I asked the leader of the French company, "How are the negotiations going?"

He responded, "The discussions are going well on the research, manufacturing, and patent areas—quite frankly, all areas except marketing." He stopped abruptly at that point.

I allowed for a pause and then asked, "Tell me more about what is not going well concerning the marketing discussions. Perhaps I can be of some help."

After what seemed like a minute, he folded his arms and tersely said, "Your company is not allowing us to help patients—more specifically mes compatriotes and fellow researchers who may need our product in the future."

Instead of immediately responding, I let that comment sit. It must be a misunderstanding, I thought, as it would be inconsistent with everything I had experienced previously to believe otherwise. While he was forthcoming, I thought it would be best if we could talk privately to more freely dissect the issue.

After the others had left the meeting room, I told him, "I understand that the product you are developing could be a big advance in cancer therapy, and we are honored to be talking with you. Please tell me more about the negotiating stalemate as it may be just a misunderstanding."

"My company must retain rights to market the product in France," he said.

"Does your company have a sales force in France or any plans for a sales force?"

"No, not given the costs involved," he said.

He seemed unwilling to go into further detail, even though it was obvious he had just stated something at best inconsistent and more typically interpreted as irrational.

"Is there something more to the story?" I asked. "Are you willing to share? Maybe I can help."

He looked me in the eye and began telling me a story about French explorers and scientists in Antarctica. I listened intently. After a few minutes of the intense narrative, he concluded, "I do not want my company to be responsible for marketing the product in France or anywhere else, as your company would be better at it. My red line is that I must ensure that the current and future scientists in French Antarctica can receive my product. If the only way to guarantee this goal is to retain commercial rights, I cannot and must not grant you worldwide commercial rights."

He was very clear that there was no negotiation around this point, no matter how irrational.

My colleague was right. It was not about money at all. His concern was that he did not trust the larger company to help the approximately twenty scientists who could potentially develop cancer while being stationed in French Antarctica. The only way he felt he could assure this was to hold onto the marketing rights in France.

"I now understand the issue," I told him. "It's important to guarantee this right so you can feel good about the deal and your fellow countrymen will always have access to your product."

He nodded. It seemed like a weight had been lifted from his shoulders.

"I think we can find other ways to make this happen without hurting the market opportunity in France for both companies," I suggested. "Do you trust me to come back with an acceptable solution?"

He nodded agreement, and we rejoined our respective negotiating teams.

I told my colleagues, "He does not want his company to market the product in France, but just wants to be assured that his product can get to his current and future countrymen, wherever they are including in French Antarctica."

They were stunned to learn of the root issue and began to Google information on French Antarctica. Of course, they would agree to permit such scientists access to the product, if needed, and this did not require the smaller company to retain marketing rights in France. After discussing it briefly within our private conference room, I suggested, "We need to open the next meeting and express our commitment to meet their needs. I am sure we can find a way to write it into our agreement with them. This should break the stalemate between our companies and allow us to finalize the agreement."

When the French company's leader heard this message, he looked over to me and smiled. The companies subsequently signed the agreement and began our partnership.

The Foundation for Success

Trust is the cornerstone of any professional or personal relationship. Without trust, society breaks down, and any element beyond the self cannot be sustained. Trust is defined as "assured reliance on the character, ability, strength, or truth of someone or something."[1] Trust is the critical enabler of our most vulnerable relations such as between a parent and child, a husband and wife, or employer and employee. It would be hard to overstate the importance of trust as it underpins almost every aspect of human interaction.

When social psychologists asked people in relationships, "What is the most desirable quality you're looking for in a partner when you're dating?" trustworthiness was the top response.[2] While partnering in the business world is quite different than dating, the attractiveness of being trustworthy is a critical characteristic for both.

Without trust, relationships, whether personal, professional, or societal, would struggle to function effectively. It would not be possible for individuals to connect, share, and collaborate on a sustainable level without having some trust within their relationships. Trust allows you to tap into a universe beyond yourself and achieve happiness, health, and success for all those involved. Like any attribute, trust can be misused and lead to significant harm to those unexpecting and vulnerable. Once lost, it is possible to restore trust, but often will take considerable time and effort.

Trust means you can count on your friend, peer, or partner to be there in difficult times, to keep promises, and to prioritize the relationship over outside influences. It promotes mutual support and commitment. I do not know how someone could get through the ups and downs of their life without having others they could confide in. Being that person for someone else will build a bond that can last a lifetime.

Trust and truth are essentially inseparable in relationships. Deception, even small lies, can erode trust quickly. Being honest about feelings, actions, and finances is critical to maintaining trust. When trust exists, friends or partners can work through conflicts more effectively, giving each other the benefit of the doubt and focusing on solutions rather than on suspicion or blame. Part of the reason this is true is that trust is usually granted when your focus is beyond just your self-interests, and you care about the other party. If you care about the other party, second chances are much easier to grant.

Being able to trust others and social systems promotes personal health as it has been shown to help alleviate hypervigilance, anxiety, and feelings of insecurity, which in turn promotes well-being.[3] Higher levels of trust raise social participation and improve an individual's subjective evaluation of quality of life.[4] Social support, facilitated by trust, has many benefits for mental and physical health. Many studies have established the benefits of social networks across the various dimensions of health and self-realization.[5] In communities, trust binds people together and creates a sense of solidarity and mutual support, which is vital during challenging times.

> ▶ Note: I have footnoted the studies without cluttering up the narrative. To read more about the information I offer, please refer to the Notes section for the appropriate citation.

Beyond a person's inner circle, the importance and difficulty to maintain a high-trust culture increases due to the high number of potential points of misunderstanding, degrees of separation, and non-trustworthy actors. Accordingly, the bar for being a trustful group or organization is not the same as for personal relationships. This reduced expectation for organizations allows them to function because it would not be possible for them to achieve the same level of trust as individual relationships.

For those organizations perceived as having trustworthy leaders, the competitive advantage in recruiting and retaining employees is significant. Research from Deloitte shows that organizations with high-trust cultures are two and a half times more likely to be high-performing revenue growth companies.[6] Organizations work diligently to become recognized as the most trusted or admired company within their industry, not just for the pats on the back, but to win with employees and partners who help the organization deliver on its business goals.

In any group or team, trust allows for open dialogue and the free exchange of ideas, which is critical for finding solutions to complex problems. When trust exists, people are more likely to support each other and contribute positively to the team. Conversely, in situations where trust is low, groups and individuals often arrive at suboptimal solutions and waste valuable time and money on ways to enforce trust, such as formal contracts, monitoring, and enforcement mechanisms—thereby significantly increasing the costs of maintaining that relationship.[7]

The costs of mistrust may become sufficiently burdensome to force the relationship to dissolve. One of the quickest ways to end negotiations with another party is to practice bad faith negotiations, breaking trust and leaving little room for a path forward. Not only will this affect the current negotiation, but future efforts as well given how reputations depend on credibility and trust.

Regarding one of the most common organizational constructs, the workplace, trust nurtures collaboration, enhances teamwork, and leads to more effective communication. Think that trust does not matter? Try meeting any of your critical organizational objectives without the support of peers, suppliers, or technical experts. Trust provides the critical link that sustains groups of people to collaborate on a common company goal.

Several studies have estimated the waste for business when employees do not have trust in each other. One such study estimated that disengagement due to low trust costs US companies approximately $450 billion to $550 billion annually.[8] Low trust not only has significant financial implications, but also discourages people from wanting to work for companies they feel they cannot trust. Since hiring has become increasingly competitive for top talent, you do not want to make it any harder on your staffing teams by developing a poor company reputation.

The correlation between trust and economic success has been well documented. In a paper by Nobel Prize–winning economist Kenneth

Arrow, he stated that "virtually every commercial transaction has within itself an element of trust, certainly any transaction conducted over a period of time."[9] Who would close a significant deal with someone they could not trust?

An economics paper by Yann Algan and Pierre Cahuc showed that there is not only a strong positive relationship between countries with higher self-reported trust attitudes and countries with higher economic activity, but also a causal relationship, suggesting that trust does indeed drive economic growth and not just correlate with it.[10] Business leaders are familiar with this insight as further validated in a survey conducted by PwC (PricewaterhouseCoopers) of 548 business executives in January 2024; 93% of business executives agreed that the ability to build and maintain trust improves the bottom line.[11] It is hard to get 93% of business executives to agree on anything, so the importance of trust must extend across the business world.

Businesses even go to great lengths to try to build trust in their products. Brand loyalty, which is built on a foundation of brand trust, plays an integral role in shaping customer behavior and influencing brand choice. Approximately 60% of customers in the US say they remain loyal to brands they trust, even if prices increase.[12] Research consistently shows trusted brands enjoy higher engagement, greater retention, and a stronger competitive edge.

A recent study by Deloitte determined that customers who trust a brand are 88% more likely to buy it again.[13] Think of products you are loyal to and trust—and probably pay more for than a similar brand. I have a trust level in Cheerios that makes it hard for me to consider alternatives despite price increases and shrinkflation (smaller boxes for the same price). Imagine the amount of money being spent to brainstorm ways to grow sales by 50% when companies should already know they just need to build a more trustworthy experience with their customers.

Beyond business organizations, trust in institutions and governments is essential for societal stability. It encourages people to follow laws, participate in civic activities, and cooperate for the common good. Governments, which depend on the support of their citizens, cannot continue to lead without proving trustworthy to some acceptable level, even in non-democratic societies. When public trust is not upheld, dissention and division are inevitable, which often lead to change in power, whether peacefully or forcefully. Recent elections have provided tremendous evidence that political parties have a long way to go to establish trust beyond their loyal followers.

Mistrust has become more common than trust in many circles, especially among political organizations. Groups enter discussions assuming the worst of intentions of their counterparts, which makes it quite difficult to reach any middle ground. Unless parties are guaranteed complete victory, an agreement on meaningful political issues remains elusive.

The inefficiency and frustration associated with operating in an environment that lacks trust results in significant costs and delays. For example, the cost of complying with federal rules and regulations in the US alone has been estimated at over $1.1 trillion—more than 10% of the GDP (Gross Domestic Product)—partly due to the lack of trust leading to excessive bureaucratic measures.[14] Unfortunately, people are too quick to blame the regulations for their problems instead of looking at the non-trustworthy actors, such as Enron, Tyco, and WorldCom, for example, which necessitated the Sarbanes-Oxley comprehensive regulations in 2002.[15]

The Bottom Line

Across personal, professional, and societal relationships, trust is not just important, it is essential. It is the foundation upon which strong, healthy relationships are built, whether between individuals, within organizations, or across society. Trust enables cooperation, fosters productivity, and ensures stability. These impacts not only improve quality of life but also the bottom line of businesses. Supported by multiple research papers and analyses, efforts to build and maintain trust are well worth it. If you are looking to prioritize your time or your company's resources on one of the most rewarding efforts you can make, it is to become more trustworthy in the eyes of your partners or employees and seek relationships with trustworthy counterparts.

Trust cannot be taken for granted, as Warren Buffett commented, "It takes twenty years to build a reputation and five minutes to ruin it."[16] Without trust, relationships deteriorate, progress stalls, and communities can fracture. The cost of mistrust is staggering when adding together all the checks and balances across society to simply try to guarantee that people will act consistently with what they have promised. Taking into account the benefits of trust and costs of mistrust, in almost every aspect of life, trust is key to success and well-being.

The So What

It would seem obvious to any organizational leader that trust is of crucial importance for success, yet making it more than an academic question requires focus and attention. When a business manager begins their day, they wrestle with issues that seem much more urgent and measurable: How can I increase revenue 5% before the end of the quarter? Why are we two months late on our planned deliverable?

The weight of these challenges occupies their full energy and concern because they need immediate resolution. Solving such problems is also why the manager has been rewarded with supervisory status and compensation. They have studied these issues in school, been mentored or advised by their management on best practices, and corrected them in the short term many times, although perhaps at a smaller and less complex scale.

In correcting the issue of the day, managers rarely go beyond the immediate symptoms of the problem. Why would they? If the company is growing and they are viewed as contributing to its success, the manager is looking at a limited time in their role, or even company, before moving on to the next role and even greater opportunity. Conversely, when opportunities are not so rosy, managers are often not invested in trying to go beyond the headline issues for an organization that does not believe in them or may not be around in a few years.

For the rare individuals who are truly invested in the organization or have the ability to tolerate short-term fires in pursuit of sustainable solutions, the state of trust across work teams and with customers becomes of paramount importance. They know that, without trust, customers will not order a product that may not address their need. They know that, without trust, a project leader will limit the exposure of mistakes that have caused significant delays. And leaders of charitable organizations know, without trust, a donor will not contribute to a worthy cause if they feel the money will simply be wasted.

How do they know? These leaders take the time to truly diagnose the problem at hand. For example, let's look at the case of a project that was not meeting its deadlines. The organizational leader would typically interview the project manager to understand their assessment of the root cause. The usual suspects include deadlines were not realistic, resources were insufficient, and other departments or suppliers had delays. The subsequent solutions range from loosening the deadlines, increasing the quantity or quality of resources, changing or penalizing supporting departments or suppliers, and abandoning the project. All of these are largely textbook and will be applied over and over.

Yet, what if the leader believed that trust was central to any organizational success? They would ask different questions and unlock important insights, likely finding out that lack of trust was the root cause of the project missing its deadline and may continue to plague the project even with new deadlines. Some questions to ask the project leader include these:

- Does the project team trust you and/or each other to fulfill their roles?
- Do you trust the suppliers to meet their obligations?
- Do you trust the project sponsor to set reasonable expectations for project deliverables? How about providing the right resources?

If you cannot trust the project leader to answer the questions honestly, that points to another problem in which trust is the fundamental issue. Assuming the project leader does answer these questions honestly, you likely have the root cause of the delays and can begin fixing them without additional delays. It could be that the sponsor and project leader was not trusted to accept realistic timelines and so the team provided aggressive timelines that they thought would be acceptable. Another reason could be that project members are not working in parallel because they do not believe their coworkers will deliver on time and so are waiting for them to finish before beginning their role.

There are many more reasons centered on lack of trust, but hopefully you get the idea. Adding more resources and extending deadlines does nothing to correct the problem and likely just rewards the low-trust environment.

Have you ever tried making a deal with another company that did not trust you? Good luck. Yet the reasons for not making the deal are rarely stated in this manner. It usually is that the other company wanted more money, the competition was too strong, or the other company really did not want to make a deal. All these reasons essentially boil down to the fact that the other company did not trust your organization to maximize the value of their asset.

Even disagreement on the valuation of an asset usually is the result of not trusting one source or another for the key assumptions. There are cases when the companies just value risk or timing differently, which has nothing to do with trust, yet if the parties trust each other enough, deal terms can usually shift the risk or timing to the party that is less risk averse or has a longer timeline with associated compensation to still make a deal possible.

When parties trust each other, deal making is so much easier and productive. A trusted partner typically (1) gets knowledge of the deal opportunity first, (2) can be more transparent in their deal assumptions to efficiently get to agreement, (3) will likely be preferred as long as their offer is in the ballpark of their competitors, and (4) will be better able to work effectively together to maximize the joint asset after the deal is done.

Reputations and word of mouth travel quickly, especially when a party is not to be trusted. In that case, the company must always outbid its competitors to have even a chance to win a competitive bid. Fortunately, as in the story of the French company concerned about scientists in French Antarctica, there is usually an opportunity to clarify misunderstandings and nip negative momentum in the bud when a leader is actively listening and engaged with the potential partner about trust.

Winning Moves

Educate your organization about how trust improves the bottom line.

- ► Make creating and maintaining trust a top priority for your organization.
- ► Diagnose organizational issues with a trust lens.
- ► Build a reputation for being a trustworthy company.
- ► Evaluate at what level of trust your relationships are with your partners and suppliers to reinforce, fix, or to exit.

2

HOW WE DEVELOP THE ABILITY TO TRUST

I COACHED YOUTH BASKETBALL AND SOCCER FOR decades for both boys and girls. I enjoyed it, not only because it provided quality time with my son and daughters on the team, but because it allowed an opportunity to help the young boys and girls grow as individuals and as a team unit. Besides knowing your son or daughter on the team, the coach usually knows only a few other friends or acquaintances when the season begins. Coaching provides a glimpse into how children and young adolescents develop the ability to trust.

I'll focus on one season in which I coached youth basketball for boys who were twelve and thirteen years old. The league was not elite in terms of talent but ultimately produced some good players for the local high school basketball teams. As usual, we worked hard on the fundamentals and tried to build skills as individuals and apply them in team strategies throughout the year, so when it came time for playoffs, we would be at our best. Team sports depend on trusting your teammates to perform their individual roles in a coordinated fashion to achieve success. It is an excellent laboratory for approaches to trust.

This particular season, we started very poorly from a win-loss record standpoint, winning only one of our first five games, but had begun turning things around entering the playoffs. As one of the lower seeds, we were forced to play some of the highest ranked teams if we were to advance in the single-game elimination tournament. Even at this level of competition and age, the excitement of the playoffs brought family members to the games whom I had never seen before, and the stands were typically full of cheering or jeering crowds.

After winning our first playoff game convincingly in an upset, we were facing a team that had lost only two games all year and was fortunate to have both great speed and rebounding. We played even for the first half and then surprised them in the third quarter by playing a trapping matchup zone once they advanced beyond half-court, which enabled us to take the lead in this closely fought contest. We were ahead by two points with about a minute to play and had to inbound the ball from underneath the basket that we were defending after the opponent had just scored and quickly called timeout.

During the timeout, I huddled the team together to provide direction and diagrammed our traditional formation on a whiteboard for such an inbounds situation. Yet it occurred to me that a traditional inbounds play is exactly what the other team would anticipate. I asked Patrick, one of our stronger players, "Do you feel confident that you can throw a pass to midcourt to Corey cutting to the basket?" Patrick gave that confident nod that confirmed I had chosen the right player.

I continued in the huddle with the entire team and said, "I believe they are going to gamble and make it very hard for us to get the ball inbounds using our normal inbounds play, which they have already seen. I want to diagram a new play that will surprise them. Do you trust each other to make it happen?"

Everyone nodded without saying a word.

I then erased the whiteboard and drew a new play on it, which involved a few picks to free up Corey for the pass at half-court. No one complained about their role or that we had not practiced it. We ended our one-minute huddle by putting one hand in a collective hands-in chant to break the huddle as the timeout ended.

So instead of the usual strategy to simply get the ball inbounds to our best foul shooter or try to wind down the clock, exactly what the other team had anticipated in setting up a defense to steal the ball, we made a pivotal change to try to score in a surprise tactic. We were able to make this decision because everyone accepted their individual responsibility and trusted each other to execute in their roles.

While such ingredients are not always reason enough for success, in this case, it worked beautifully as we stunned the other team and scored to put the game out of reach. The play further reinforced our belief in each other, and we subsequently won the remaining three playoff games to win the championship that year.

Our Journey with Trust

Trust is a word that is universally known, even though individual definitions may differ, largely due to experience. Those experiences, both positive and negative, make trust one of the most emotionally charged words in our language. Trust does not wait until we are fully mature for those experiences, and we continue to refine our association with trust throughout our lives.

As an important trait for survival, we learn the concept of trust early in life, regardless of location, gender, or race. How a person develops the ability to trust is not only important to understand when interacting with kids, but also with people who come from different backgrounds. Although it should be obvious, we cannot assume that everyone had similar experiences as ourselves growing up, whether a dependable set of parents, safe home, or supportive neighborhood, and acknowledging that reality will prove useful as we consider how to approach trust-based relationships with others.

Developmental psychologists emphasize that the foundation of trust is typically established in infancy and early childhood. This initial development of trust is largely influenced by the child's relationship with their primary caregivers, generally parents. Erik Erikson, a renowned developmental psychologist, proposed that the first stage of his psychosocial development theory, known as Trust vs. Mistrust, occurs in infancy (from birth to around eighteen months). During this stage, consistent and reliable caregiving fosters a sense of trust in the infant. If caregivers provide a nurturing and predictable environment, the child learns to trust others and feels secure. Conversely, inconsistent or neglectful caregiving can lead to mistrust and insecurity.[17]

Noted British psychologist and psychiatrist John Bowlby contributed insights that children are born with an innate need for secure and meaningful relationships with their mothers. This relationship will encourage positive cognitive and emotional development that helps them survive into adulthood.[18] Children begin to differentiate between trustworthy and untrustworthy sources around age three, refining this ability by age five. Social interactions during these ages play a significant role in shaping trust beliefs. Trust is no longer centered on the caregiver but expands to others with whom the child interacts.

In one landmark study of trust within childhood, Lucy Betts, Ken Rotenberg, and Mark Trueman examined young children between the ages of five and seven, with participants having a mean age of slightly over six years old. They found that children with low generalized trust had fewer friends than their peers who had higher generalized trust.[19] In a similar study, Rotenberg and others found a negative relationship between trust beliefs and loneliness from early childhood to adulthood.[20] In other words, trust is necessary for friendships, even early in life.

Additional studies have shown that a child's evaluation of trust has great influence on their future prosocial behaviors, defined as actions to help or benefit others. In one study, Tina Malti and others studied 1,675 first graders who were seven years old at the beginning of the study and found a relationship between the trustworthiness of a child and that child's prosocial behaviors, such as helping or sharing.[21] Children who were evaluated as trustworthy by their peers and teachers exhibited higher levels of prosocial behaviors than children who were evaluated as less trustworthy.

Another study by Rotenberg and colleagues examined the relationship between trust beliefs and prosocial behaviors, especially the helpfulness of children in grades five and six, which corresponded to a mean age of ten. They found a significant correlation between children's trust beliefs and their helpfulness to their classmates.[22]

As children grow into adolescence, they engage with a broader range of social contexts and diverse groups of people. Children and adolescents develop a more nuanced understanding of trust and its implications as their interactions increase, and they can learn from their experiences. This exposure can challenge their ability to find shared interests and norms, which may affect their trust of individuals beyond their family.

With greater interactions and an increasing focus on peer relationships, social reputations develop, which further help or hinder the ability to offer or receive trust. The explosion of social media has augmented and sometimes replaced in-person interactions among peer groups, which can lead to accelerated and exaggerated trust outcomes. People may not be mature enough to send or receive messages on social media, which further complicates trust signaling and interpretation.[23]

Older adolescents, from age fifteen to nineteen, tend to be less naive and more skeptical in their judgments about people due to any past disappointments and their cognitive development.[24] Based on surveys of 1,535 adolescents collected over two years, scientists found that middle and late adolescents had significantly lower levels of trust than early adolescents and that these beliefs became more grounded and less related to interpersonal trust than in early adolescence. This reduced level of trust continues into adulthood.

By the time you are an adult, your willingness to trust others can be quite constrained if your past experiences were etched with relationships that were not supportive or predictable. Unfortunately, some of the most poignant and lasting lessons concerning trust come from relationships that start out with trust as an important component and then fall apart due to a break in that trust. Like most behaviors, trust can be strongly reinforced or constrained through experiences and relationships in which trust was at risk.

Studies suggest that individuals develop a firm understanding of trust that may be harder to change by the time they reach adulthood. However, psychologists using trust games have shown that adults can adjust their trust levels based on the behavior of others.[25] This adaptability indicates that trust and distrust are not fixed traits and can change based on interpersonal experiences throughout your adult life. The degree and ease of change depends greatly on the circumstances and past experiences of the individuals involved.

The Bottom Line

A person's ability to trust and distrust starts early in childhood through experiences with their primary caregiver and evolves throughout their life. As your social interactions increase beyond your family and peer relationships grow in their importance, you will live through positive and negative experiences that either reinforce or break previous assumptions about trust. Relationships with family, friends, and coworkers, along with the growing influence of social media, will help shape someone's willingness to trust and refine their norms for being trustworthy. These direct and indirect influences combined with personal experiences continually shape our ability to trust throughout our life.

The So What

Why should you care how a child develops the ability to trust if you are managing an organization of adults? Well, for one, we all interact with children at some point in our adult life, whether our own, extended family, neighbors, or as professionals (in roles such as teacher, coach, or company that supports children). In such roles, it is critical to establish solid trust relationships and build a healthy appreciation and practice of trust for the child's well-being.

Much more relevant for business leaders, knowing how people develop their ability to trust is highly relevant because the roots of trust profoundly shape how adults interact in organizations, make decisions, and respond to leadership. Trust isn't just situational—it's developmental. The way individuals learned to trust (or not) in childhood influences how they approach authority, collaboration, and risk-taking in their adult professional life.

People with early positive trust experiences tend to be more open to teamwork, innovation, and feedback. This includes employees, volunteers, peers, and leaders. While it may be difficult to know the background of any individual employee, a leader should not assume that everyone's childhood experience was like their own.

Leaders who understand how trust is developed can better tailor their approach to employees with different backgrounds. Today's workforce is much more diverse than in past years, in which some general assumptions may have held. With a workforce that spans generations, each shaped by evolving patterns of media consumption, news events, and varying degrees of social trust, past best practices may no longer prove helpful. Despite these challenges, a leader can still refine their approach to trust without stooping to stereotypes and hearsay, which will quickly undermine the credibility of the leader and perpetuate hurtful falsehoods.

If a leader learns directly from an employee about challenges in their upbringing, or if the organization operates within a cultural community where strong parenting is less common, the leader should approach trust building with greater patience and intentionality. This fine-tuning in their approach helps leaders create environments that rebuild or reinforce trust for those who may have grown up without strong trust models. Without this understanding, leaders may misinterpret employee hesitation, resistance, or disengagement as incompetence, when it may stem from deeply ingrained trust patterns. Knowing how trust forms helps leaders create sustainable strategies to strengthen trust at all levels—manager to employee, team to team, and company to customer.

It takes time to mentor others, yet it can be an incredibly enabling experience for the mentee when the mentor is not just checking a box in support of a scorecard for human resources. Trust is the ideal topic to go over each time you meet as it is a key barometer of organizational relationships that will empower career advancement and further net-working—exactly what mentees tend to have the most interest in.

Before engaging in the dialogue around trust, you should ensure a common understanding of what trust means to each of you. Exchanging your views on trust level-sets to correct for differences in how each experienced and developed the ability to trust. You can pull examples from your experiences, both good and bad, to reinforce the importance of trust and its role in making complex efforts possible.

Shifting beyond a one-on-one interaction to leading an organization, the culture of an organization can be a tremendous ally (or enemy, if destructive in nature) to help employees of different backgrounds develop a common appreciation of trust. Recognizing that trust is learned behavior helps leaders intentionally shape organizational culture to be an environment where people feel safe, valued, and empowered.

Leaders need to check the pulse of their organizational culture to understand if it is reinforcing the right behavior or seeding doubt and conflict. Even for small teams, like the basketball team that I coached, trust can be a critical enabler to success when the leader nurtures trust and engages in experiences that further build and reinforce existing trust. Asking the team if they trusted each other can be high risk, yet when a leader has the pulse of their team, it can elevate the team culture to new levels of sustainability.

A leader cannot be naive to their team attitudes or ignore warning signs. Changing a negative team environment requires swift and clear action to remove bad influences and send an unambiguous signal to the remaining members. Otherwise, the leader will be facing an uphill battle on trust for quite some time, which will reappear as missed deadlines, unmet expectations, and poor results.

Winning Moves

Don't assume everyone developed trust as you did. Be open to people where they are in their trust journey and refine leadership actions as a result.

- ► Ensure that children with whom you have influence experience healthy trust relationships.
- ► Model and teach trust skills to others, especially as a mentor.
- ► Monitor organizational culture to ensure it is an ally—and correct swiftly if not.

3

WHOM WE TRUST AND WHY

N 2007, MY SON AND HIS friends were on their way to achieving Eagle Scout status, which is the highest rank within the Boy Scouts system. One of the desired experiences in accomplishing that goal is to participate in a high-adventure camp. The scout is placed in a real-world setting designed to push past their comfort zone and help them understand who they are and envision who they can become.

This was not going to be a story in which I was involved until the leader of the expedition had to cancel a few weeks before the trip. Faced with the cancellation of the expedition, which would be a significant setback for the adolescents, I was volunteered, while away on a business trip, to lead the group of seven teenage boys on this adventure. I was not volunteered due to my camping expertise. Quite the opposite, as I am better suited for business travel at Marriott hotels, yet the parents of the scouts trusted that I would make the right decisions and could lead the boys to succeed in the mission.

While the parents had trust in me, the scouts had only limited exposure to me, besides my son. To get a sense of our capabilities and build some rapport, I scheduled a get-together with the boys a week before we were to set out, in which we would review our plans and supplies and have a test run canoeing in a local park. This was an opportunity to build trust and worked quite well until I tipped over one of the canoes.

Although we quickly righted the canoe, I know this did not instill great confidence among the scouts. I did not get upset or blame others for the mishap and voiced that it was my bad. I explained how I became distracted and caused the weight imbalance and that I would learn from it. I knew some events on the trip were not going to go as planned and hoped my reaction to my mistake could help set a tone that this trip was not about perfection but growing as an individual and group. The other parents who had been watching gave me a thumbs-up, potentially due to the lack of alternative options.

About a week later, we departed for our high-adventure outing. We were bused for a few hours to the Adirondacks in northern New York with our backpacks, tents, clothing, and food for the week. We soon met the eighth member of our group, an engineering student at a nearby college, who volunteered to help with high-adventure outings in the mountains. Besides balancing the troop, he was helpful and became the second adult if I needed to leave the group to provide medical help with any of the scouts.

Our mission was to travel from our drop-off point at Hoel Pond and, with the use of four canoes and our hiking shoes, navigate rivers, climb small mountains, and hike about twenty miles to reach a rendezvous destination at Lake Saranac in six days. We would have access only to what we could carry on our backs to eat, sleep, and shelter in. Given that each person was to carry about 20% of their weight or at most thirty-five pounds, not including when portaging the canoes, meant that we would need to rely on each other to carry items meant for the entire group. Trust was built into this mission by its design. It is another level of trust when only one person carries the day's meal or week's toilet paper for the group.

I assigned roles to each of the scouts based upon a quick assessment of their capabilities and interest, such as being responsible for making sure cooking fires were lit, subsequently putting the fire out, orienteering consistent with our map, and securing the bear bag at night. In this way, everyone was essential and contributing to our group's success. I had responsibilities, too, as to build sustainable trust, a leader needs to be viewed as a member of the team.

One of the more difficult discussions was around toilet paper. I announced to the scouts, "Just like every other resource that we have, we cannot all carry toilet paper in our backpacks in order to make room for everything that we have to carry. We need to assign one person to carry it for our entire team." The groans across the boys were obvious. Unlike peanut butter, the water purifier, and other essentials that we had already assigned volunteers to carry for the troop, toilet paper hit home and everyone wanted to be the one to carry it.

I made another plea, "Is the responsibility for the water purifier any less important than the toilet paper? Come on, guys." That seemed to resonate with many of them and the mutiny was called off.

I then decided to announce, "I am going to assign Andrew, our most senior scout, to carry the toilet paper for all of us." I looked at Andrew and publicly asked him, "Andrew, can we trust you with this important responsibility?"

He did not blink an eye and immediately responded, "Of course." That was the end of the toilet paper issue.

The trip proceeded well, yet I was unable to execute one of my planned tasks—giving nightly reports to the parents at home—as cell phone strength was too weak for much of the trip. It did not affect our journey, but it likely caused additional anxiety for some of the parents.

While I was granted significant license to lead given that I was the adult in the room, teenage boys can quickly prove unruly if they view situations as being unfair or moving toward disaster. I gained their trust and built upon it by being consistent in my decision-making, not playing favorites, being committed to the group success, and being honest about my own strengths and weaknesses. I was happy to delegate orienteering and cooking to others and enjoyed the views from the last canoe. When we lost our only fishing pole after a few hours into our trip, I handled it much like my own tipping of the canoe a week prior—let's learn from it and move on.

We encountered other challenges such as when beavers dammed a waterway that we had intended to use and when fatigue caused us to take twice the time planned for portage of our canoes. Of greater concern, with only a few days left in our trip, our water filtering pump broke. While each of us recognized the impact of this setback, we did not whine about it but solved it as a group to use chemical tablets, our backup plan, which we entrusted to one of the scouts to carry.

To keep morale high, we took one night off to relax and jump off a small cliff into a deep section of the lake. Most importantly, throughout all the adventures, the scouts trusted each other and grew as individuals, while building memories that will last a lifetime.

The Trust Decision

Have you ever wondered why someone seems to be trusting of others despite clear signs of concern? Or how someone decides to trust a colleague and not yourself? While we develop the ability to trust others early in life, the actual decision to trust another person involves a complex interplay of cognitive and emotional processes along with any past experiences between the trustor (the person deciding to trust) and the trustee (the person being trusted).

The personality and emotions of the trustor, such as whether they tend to be gregarious or introverted, and the context of the trustee, are they aggressively pursuing a quick sale, come into play during this multifaceted process. Understanding the key elements that drive such decisions can help explain why trust decisions can be different across individuals and situations. Recognizing these factors in advance of interactions can greatly increase the odds of a successful relationship. For example, a highly disciplined accountant may be slow to trust a disorganized fashion designer.

Using experiments to better understand the decision-making process, researchers concluded that several factors relating to the trustor play a pivotal role in the decision to trust someone. First, trust decisions can be driven by both impulsive and deliberate processes. Impulsive trust is often automatic and emotion-based and can be as simple as I just like the way she presents herself, while deliberative trust involves careful consideration of factors such as risk, the trustee's ability, benevolence, and integrity. The context of the interaction can determine which process dominates, although decisions of greater risk tend to follow a deliberate process.[26]

Beyond the process chosen, several personal characteristics of the trustor influence trust decisions including an individual's general tendency to trust others, a trustor's current emotional state, and their cognitive abilities to evaluate trustworthiness accurately, among others.[27] For example, if the trustor is in a good mood, they are more likely to trust others than when feeling down. In addition, people who score higher in being agreeable, open, and conscientious are more likely to trust strangers. In the absence of direct information about a stranger, our trust decisions often reflect our own personality traits rather than objective assessments.[28]

Research shows that people often trust strangers because they feel a sense of moral duty or social responsibility to do so, even if they're unsure about the stranger's trustworthiness. This sense of obligation that some people feel helps to maintain social order and enables cooperation in society, making activities like commerce or public transportation possible.[29] Unfortunately, this trusting behavior also can result in tragedy in rare circumstances, such as the murder of "Good Samaritan" Paul Clifford in December, 2024.[30]

People frequently assess strangers based on their resemblance to people they have previously known. Either consciously or unconsciously, if a stranger reminds you of someone trustworthy from your past, you are more likely to extend trust to them. This is referred to as a Pavlovian learning mechanism in which moral information from past experiences guides our future choices.[31]

Trust decisions also vary across countries. Fortunately, a widely accepted tool to measure trust attitudes can be found in the World Values Survey (WVS), an international research program devoted to the scientific and academic study of social, political, economic, religious, and cultural values of people in the world. Started in 1981, the organization has been operating in more than 120 countries and conducts surveys every five years.[32]

The WVS asks many different questions about trust. While imperfect, it provides informative data across countries that has been collected for decades. A key measure assessed in the survey is this statement: "Most people can be trusted." Respondents from all but four countries agreed with that statement less than 50%, with Sweden the highest at

64%, Uganda the lowest at 8%, and the US at 36%. Another trust-related question measured agreement with the statement: "Most people would try to take advantage of you." The results were consistent with Sweden being the lowest with only 12% agreeing with the statement, Turkey the highest at 78%, and the US at 37%.

Initially, you might think that most of the world is quite untrusting based on these results. Yet there is much more nuance to people's attitudes. When the WVS asked for agreement with the statement, "How much do you trust people in your neighborhood?" survey respondents had much higher trust scores with most countries well above 60%, including Norway, Sweden, Germany, Finland, and Denmark above 90% and the US at 84%. You can surmise that familiarity plays a very distinct role in trust and that, absent of that familiarity, trust is significantly lower.

The Bottom Line

Deciding to trust someone is a multifaceted process influenced by many factors, using both impulsive and deliberate processes. Several personal characteristics of the trustor influence trust decisions including an individual's general tendency to trust others, a trustor's current emotional state, and their cognitive abilities to evaluate trustworthiness accurately. Trustors often trust complete strangers due to a sense of social obligation and resemblance to people that they have previously trusted.

The environment in which the interaction takes place also has a great degree of influence on whether trust is granted. In most countries, including the US, people did not generally agree that others can be trusted. However, when the location of the person to be trusted was familiar, the response became much more positive. While the trustor has natural tendencies, including location, that influence their ability to grant trust, the behavior of the trustee cannot be underestimated within this equation.

The So What

Any effort is easier if the people involved trust each other. Gaining that initial trust can prove challenging, so that is why it is crucial to create an environment that increases the odds that you will be trusted. While most of the time you will deal with people you already know and can leverage past joint experiences to fuel being trusted (such as the scouts on our adventure trip; they trusted me and so did their parents), people who don't know you can be critical to your success as well. How to get them to give you the benefit of the doubt needs to be thoughtful and not just left to chance.

Let's use an example to drive this point home. In a scenario in which you are leading a not-for-profit organization that is raising funds and you have your first appointment with a targeted high-net-worth individual, the potential donor needs to trust you or your organization to ultimately contribute to your cause. The potential donor will likely have some perceptions coming into the meeting from word of mouth, friends, or research. Ideally, all these sources would support an image of high trust in your organization, but it takes significant time and energy to build a broad reputation, and you may not be there yet.

Instead of relying on sources of information beyond your control, you should provide the potential donor with credible information as to why they should trust your organization with their funds. A common friend or mutual contact to introduce you would be ideal, yet sometimes you need to build that trust from scratch. Combining the data with probing questions that help you understand what the potential donor cares about allows you to customize the presentation in a meaningful way. While showing that you care about the donor through such questions, you are also better able to respect their time by disregarding information that they do not care about. This begins to build a trustworthy relationship. Perhaps you only need to show the donor information about other organizations that have contributed based on your discussion, instead of data about the prudent use of any donated funds or controls in place.

When you involve a mutual friend or contact, the donor's trust in that relationship can naturally flow to your organization, assuming it was a positive relationship. This is the optimal approach before meeting the first time and a highly time-tested and proven strategy. However, in many cases such a contact may not be available or you are not sure that the relationship was something that you want associated with your organization. In that case, sending information directly to the potential donor in the hope of obtaining a meeting may be the only option to initiate a trusting environment.

You probably do not want to meet with the potential donor during a natural disaster, right before a business deadline, the last day before they leave on vacation, or during a time in which they are highly stressed as they will likely not be able to give you the attention that you want, even if they agree to meet. While you may benefit from the distraction or the donor being overcome with emotion in the short term, a sustainable relationship does not take advantage of such influences. Try to create an environment as close to normal as possible in a comfortable location that is consistent with the persona of your organization. To the degree the meeting place is close to the potential donor has the benefit of convenience but, more importantly, takes advantage of the natural tendency to trust others from familiar locations.

Finally, when the meeting takes place, you need to act consistently with the expectations for the meeting: Show up on time, cover the agreed upon agenda, and be willing to end on time. You can certainly extend the meeting if the potential donor agrees, yet you are working to limit any surprises that would reduce trust. I will cover the qualities of a trustworthy person in detail in the next chapter as the focus here is more on creating the right environment to gain trust in an initial meeting.

This example could just as easily be a key customer, someone's boss, or potential business partner. What really matters is that you think through any common relationships and the timing, setting, and pre-meeting perceptions when meeting someone for the first time so you can increase the odds that you will develop a trusting relationship. Obviously, things do not always go to plan and you may need multiple meetings to accomplish what you hope for in the first meeting, yet the planning and effort will pay off over time if the parties have a mutual interest in a relationship.

I know that was the case in our high-adventure scouting trip. Tipping the canoe was not what I envisioned for our test run, yet it provided a very real opportunity to establish how we would work together during our adventure. In responding to the mistake with humility and responsibility, I demonstrated trustworthy behaviors that were more important than being an expert in canoeing.

With careful planning, patience, and perseverance, a leader can build a trusted relationship that results in much more than great memories, potentially even transforming a company or developing its next CEO.

Winning Moves

Recognize that people will decide whether to trust or not in different ways than you do.

- ▶ Control your bias to not determine the trustworthiness of a person based on resemblance to another.
- ▶ Don't let a bad day or mood affect your evaluation of someone else.
- ▶ If the other person is rushed or dealing with significant concerns, ask them if your meeting should be rescheduled to give your relationship the best chance.
- ▶ Build a strong and trusted network of people who can then introduce you to other people you may need to work with.
- ▶ Prioritize demonstrating trustworthy behaviors when meeting people the first time.

4

A PRACTICAL FRAMEWORK FOR MAKING BETTER DECISIONS

THE COMPANY I WORKED FOR WAS at a pivotal time. They had just decided to withdraw a billion-dollar product from the market, which had been a key growth driver, and many of their largest products were mature with declining revenues. Just in time, the company's scientists and clinicians had developed a novel and first-in-class product candidate that likely would be approved for use in patients with type 2 diabetes within three years. I was charged with leading the pre-launch commercial strategy and launch execution for this product, and there was significant pressure to succeed.

We were entering a disease category that had reached epidemic proportions with a disease prevalence of over 11% of the US population, almost 30% in seniors over sixty-five, and the eighth leading cause of death with direct and indirect medical costs of over $400 billion as of 2023.[33] Many companies had been assisting physicians and patients for years in the fight against diabetes, so being a new company entering such an entrenched and competitive area was going to be difficult.

The strategy I developed had been reviewed, refined, and approved by senior management several times, and we felt we would be successful if the product continued to perform well in clinical trials. The strategy incorporated some innovations, especially concerning the application of an omnichannel (seamless, high-quality customer experiences across print, digital, and in-person channels) communication program, which was unique for that time but was largely applying existing best practices at scale and a brand positioning of add-on treatment that market research made obvious. We would need to execute the strategy with minimal surprises to ensure launch success.

I continued to seek something more, being endlessly curious and unsatisfied with the current state of patient challenges in trying to live with diabetes. We sought and gained permission through a market research vendor to visit with some of the patients in various parts of the country and within their homes to try to tease out something else that could make a difference for them. That research and other observations began to point to something potentially noteworthy.

It turns out that diabetes is one of the few diseases—given the tremendous personal and societal costs—in which there are specific educators who teach patients how to better manage the disease. These educators, called Certified Diabetes Educators (CDEs), help diabetes patients develop a personalized treatment plan to manage their blood glucose levels and practice how to monitor and manage their levels, explaining what to do if they get low. There are about 19,000 of these health professionals, of which many are nurses. This insight became important as CDEs can make a big difference in terms of the patient experience with a diabetes product.

Doing more extensive research, we understood that this professional community was tremendously under-resourced, often making their patient materials at home at their own cost. Everyone had their own set of materials such as handouts, and they often were quite worn out. There seemed to be an opportunity to help them do their jobs better.

While we were reviewing the market research, one of my direct reports and another colleague met a start-up company that was developing visual maps that conveyed diabetes information that could be useful for patients. They introduced me to the company, and I looked at their three-by-five-foot prototype map and saw tremendous potential. These maps could be used in interactive group settings led by the CDE, where approximately ten patients at each session could learn from each other as well. After talking to the executives at this company, I felt that they could scale and deliver training that would make a big difference in patient education. We needed to be hands-off the materials to avoid any chance that people would perceive us having any self-serving influence, so we discussed turning this education development over to the American Diabetes Association (ADA), a leader in the diabetes community.

This was the program that could serve as a true partnership with the medical community. The goal would be to provide these materials to all the CDEs, along with training on how to use them with patients within the first few years of our product launch. While it was nice to have uncovered this idea, proving to management and getting their support could not be assumed. This was a complex and ambitious plan, something the company had never done before, which contained a myriad of risks, including potentially hurting the launch of our diabetes product.

I prepared the necessary arguments, projections, budgets, and pros and cons in presenting to senior management. They understood the potential to dramatically improve patient education but also the risks with a program this novel and complex during our launch. At the end of the final review meeting, they seemed to be on the fence as to whether to approve.

The last question from one executive was, "Are you confident that you will be able to pull it off?"

I told him, "While I don't think anyone has done something like this before at scale, I feel confident. I trust my team based on who they are and what they've done and because the environment, specifically the medical community, should be extremely supportive of such an effort. Yes, we can make this happen."

At the end of the meeting, the senior VP said, "You have our trust. Please move forward and keep us posted on any additional support you need." I could not have asked for a better outcome.

It turned out to be a wise decision. The company funded high-quality educational materials and training sessions that trained over 15,000 CDEs, more than 75% of the total, within two years and helped standardize diabetes patient education across the country. Over a million patients received that education, which helped them to better understand their disease and ways to improve their health. It also helped our company become a leader in diabetes solutions. Not to be forgotten, the product that we launched was viewed by financial analysts as one of the most successful launches ever in the industry.

From Gut to Great

When executives sit in the boardroom trying to decide whether to trust another company or leader, they can consider many variables and scenarios to agree upon a decision, yet it rarely follows a scripted approach. Everyone likely has their own rubric for making such a decision, with many relying on a gut feeling or simply experience. If asked, it would be surprising if most people could articulate how they came to the choice whether to trust someone who was not within their inner circle. While intuitive thought processes can sometimes lead to better answers than systemic thinking, studies show that you increase your chances of making the best decision using proven, structured decision processes.[34]

So why do people rely on their gut to make such important decisions? It usually comes down to what is easiest and most expedient. For decisions that have little downside or resource costs—such as whether to trust a server's recommendation for the veal scallopini at a restaurant—it makes a lot of sense to not go through an extensive decision-making process. However, for decisions that may involve longer term tradeoffs—like the choice to trust to invest resources in a new business line such as mine for diabetes education—rigorous data-driven decision rubrics are well worth the effort.

Given the need for an effective decision-making tool that can incorporate the strengths of simplicity and speed while applying critical structured aspects to guide an informed decision regarding trust, I have developed the Trustworthy Decision Matrix. This matrix requires only two variables: (1) the track record of the person or company in meeting expectations, and (2) the degree of difficulty of the project or task being undertaken. Visually, it looks like this:

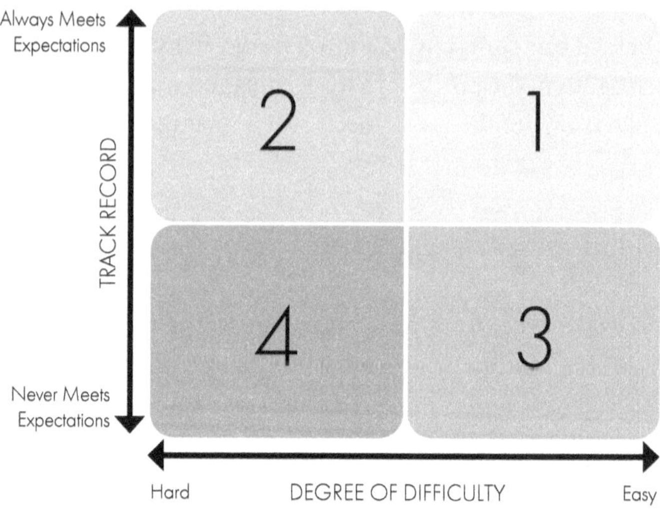

I labeled the four different quadrants 1 through 4 and will assign them names after discussing them. The numbering relates to the desirability of moving forward and trusting the person or company to complete the task or project being contemplated. The decision to move forward and trust the person or company on the task or project increases as the matrix goes from the bottom left to upper right of the matrix.

Quadrant 1 will be labeled as "Go Forward." In this scenario, the person or company has a track record of always meeting expectations and the degree of difficulty for the project or task is easy, from the perspective of the environment being supportive, the project or task having been done successfully before, and the person or company having the requisite skill set and resources. For example, the decision to trust the Hershey Company to produce a new candy bar would be placed in the first quadrant or Go Forward. Hershey has an excellent track record of producing millions of candy bars in the past, and they have a supportive environment, skills, and resources to do it again. Please note that producing a candy bar is far from easy for most of us, but the determination of being easy is relative to the person or company being evaluated.

Quadrant 4 will be labeled "No Go." In this scenario, the person or company has a track record of not meeting expectations, and the task or project is viewed as hard. For this example, let's imagine that I contracted with a kitchen remodeler who was late in completing the project, cost well over the agreed upon budget, and aspects of the kitchen were of mixed quality such as the cabinets that did not tightly close, thereby not meeting my expectations. After finishing the remodeling project, the contractor informed me of a new venture that he was entering, that of landscape design, and asked me if I would be interested in trusting him to update my front yard.

Using the Trustworthy Decision Matrix, the answer would be a "No Go." Not only does the contractor have a poor track record, but for him the project would be difficult because he has not done this work before and he doesn't have the skills or resources to support success in this new venture.

The intermediate quadrants are less obvious, but still straightforward to think through. We'll go back to Hershey as a company that meets expectations, which places them either in quadrant 1 or 2. In this example, let's assume that instead of producing a new candy bar, they have a project to produce a new pizza, perhaps a chocolate-covered pizza. Producing a new pizza would be easy for Domino's, but Hershey likely does not have the experience, expertise, or resources available to support such an effort. So even though the company is quite trustworthy, it would be difficult to go forward because the obstacles for Hershey to overcome are significant.

I have labeled this number 2 quadrant "Proceed Dependent on Additional Support" because you still may be tempted to bet on Hershey to succeed given their track record, but given the degree of difficulty, Hershey will need additional expertise or resources to be trusted to meet expectations in this new challenge. Without such support, there is a significant likelihood of failure as trust does not extend indefinitely to areas in which the person or company does not have experience.

For the final scenario, we will go back to the kitchen contractor as an example of a company that we have little, if any, trust in. This lack of trust relegates any new decision involving them to either quadrant 3 or 4, depending on how easy the project is viewed. As an example, let's assume that the project was to repair the cabinetry that he had installed a few years ago. Given his expertise and working experience with the cabinetry, this should be an easy task for him. I have labeled this number 3 quadrant as "Decline Unless Low Risk" because the poor track record of the kitchen contractor makes it unlikely that I would be pleased with all aspects of his work. However, if the downside of potential delays, higher costs, and low quality would have a minimal impact to me, I could move forward and trust him to do so. Otherwise, I should simply decline reengaging with the kitchen contractor on this new effort.

Like any tool that tries to simplify and expedite decision processes, the complexity and importance of the decision being evaluated may necessitate a much more thorough and thoughtful decision process. Still, this tool should have good utility for the many situations that arise in which you need to make a timely decision to trust someone, or some organization and the stakes involved are manageable. The full Trustworthy Decision Matrix is depicted here:

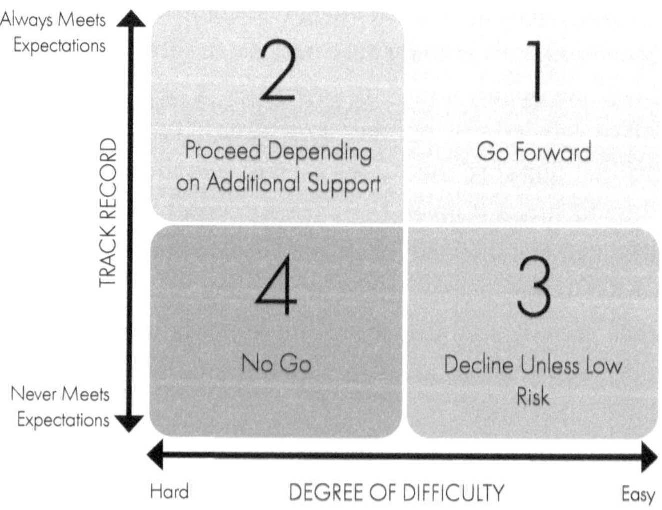

The Bottom Line

The Trustworthy Decision Matrix provides a simple and powerful tool to frame and evaluate many trust decisions. The matrix requires only two variables: (1) the track record of the person or company in meeting expectations, and (2) the degree of difficulty of the project or task being undertaken. Based upon the results of your evaluation of these variables, go or no-go trust decisions are made.

The matrix rewards trustworthy employees by assigning them to both easy and difficult projects, provided the necessary resources are available. In contrast, untrustworthy employees are restricted from challenging assignments, independent of resource availability.

The So What

Personnel decisions will make or break the success of a manager. While you will do everything you can to hire superstars, you will inevitably manage some direct reports or team members who do not consistently meet expectations. As a leader, you may receive some empathy, but there is no room to compromise on delivering results. Beyond this reality, the best leaders simultaneously develop organizational capabilities and talent while achieving objectives—assuming, of course, that not everything is outsourced.

How do you decide who should lead a project? Sometimes your choices can be easy such as deploying a successful team leader to perform a critical project almost identical to the one they had just completed. Most situations are not straightforward and require judgment in making tradeoffs on personnel and non-human assets. The ability to make informed decisions using an objective and transparent process reduces risk, increases buy-in from those involved, and facilitates long-term planning of resources. While it does not guarantee that the result will be better than a pure gut decision, chances are quite high that a decision-making tool will not only produce at least an equal outcome, but a systematic decision process will also build a more supportive organization.

The Trustworthy Decision Matrix is that decision support tool. It allows the leader to frame the decision on a few variables that should be readily available: the track record of an employee, the relative difficulty of the project, the risk associated with the project, and resources available to support the project team.

If I have trust in an employee based on their history of completing projects successfully, I feel confident in giving them an easy assignment, such as one similar to what they have already accomplished. Many projects will be assigned in this manner for most organizations.

Yet, how comfortable should I be in giving them a new assignment that is difficult or different from what they have previously experienced? Many managers would use their gut and simply assign the project to this trustworthy performer. Conventional management theory would have a hard time saying such a decision is wrong. However, the Trustworthy Decision Matrix adds the requirement that the project should not be assigned to them unless there are supportive resources that can assist the project leader.

The rationale for requiring supportive resources is to reduce the risk of this difficult project being unsuccessful and to further develop a trustworthy project leader for even more challenging assignments. What additional resources are we talking about? It can range from simple steps, such as increased senior oversight or regular check-ins with the project leader, to more complex measures, such as auditing each milestone to validate progress and make course corrections. Such resources depend on the current strengths and weaknesses of the project leader and the specific needs of the project. Being trustworthy is not evaluated as a strength or weakness because to even get into this decision bucket, you need to be trustworthy.

Developing a trustworthy employee is an important byproduct of the Trustworthy Decision Matrix. By demonstrating to a manager that you are willing to trust them on a difficult project, you are increasing loyalty with your most dependable employees while also furthering their engagement and skill base. They will likely socialize this feeling with other employees and continue to promote a positive work environment.

However, if they sense they are just being set up to fail in being assigned a difficult project, versus being assigned tools and help to succeed, this growth opportunity could break trust and lead the employee to lose trust in the organization. If you truly have a superstar employee who rises to every challenge given them, it may not matter if any support is provided for a particular project. Inevitably, at some higher level or project complexity, it will matter. Also, the signal that you are modeling for this trustworthy employee and the organization is far from a best practice in employee development and retention.

While it is easier to talk about the trustworthy employee, not everyone we work with consistently delivers on expectations. For these employees, assigning them a difficult project will likely result in significant waste of time and money. It also takes away a growth opportunity from a trustworthy employee who may be available. No additional resources should be expended to try to help this project leader succeed as their track record leads you to predict this assignment may be simply prolonging the inevitable disappointment.

Project leaders or employees who are not trustworthy should either not have meaningful roles in your organization or be assigned to work on relatively easy and non-critical efforts. They will still likely underperform, but it is the most practical use of limited resources. If they are observed to be not trustworthy later in their career and are working in a pivotal role, they need to be removed from that role or the organization as soon as feasible. Trust is difficult to build and maintain in an organization, and you need to act decisively when it is threatened or weakened by individuals, regardless of seniority.

Therefore, what do you do when you only have one person available to lead or perform a difficult or high-risk project and they happen to be untrustworthy? You are best to postpone the project until you can find a trustworthy employee to lead it or outsource the project. Otherwise, you should find another way to solve whatever the project was meant to deliver for the organization. Trusting someone who has proven to be not trustworthy simply is not a viable strategy.

The Trustworthy Decision Matrix structures decisions in a simple yet meaningful way to systematically improve decision-making, allocate resources, and assure project success. While its sophistication may be underwhelming to some, by reducing complex problems to a few straightforward variables, its ease of use, practicality, and transparency makes its highly valuable and executable. It will also result in an organization that places greater value in being trustworthy, which should elevate the bottom line of even the highest performing companies.

I am fortunate that my senior management had the gut instincts at the time we were launching into the diabetes market to give the go-ahead to move forward with the project and provide additional resources. This is exactly the same outcome that they would have come to using the Trustworthy Decision Matrix. Instead of relying upon pure judgment that you will just know the best thing to do, please use the matrix to improve your decision-making and increase the likelihood of success. Your teams will greatly appreciate and benefit from its use.

Winning Moves

Assess how you make decisions regarding trust.

- ▶ Try the Trustworthy Decision Matrix to validate your decisions or make new ones.
- ▶ Do not keep taking risks with untrustworthy employees.
- ▶ Reward your trustworthy team members with growth opportunities.
- ▶ Apply your limited resources to trustworthy talent.

5

THE SEVEN CHARACTERISTICS OF TRUSTWORTHY PEOPLE

WHEN I WAS THE GLOBAL HEAD of the eye therapeutic business for a leading pharmaceutical company, we were exploring ways to augment our internal pipeline with products being developed by other companies. Without a novel product to add to our portfolio, we could not deliver on our strategic vision and the desired profitability for the company. On everyone's minds was the reality that we risked not having the size and scale to justify a relaunch of our US sales force and the number of employees within headquarters without finding a product that had the potential to be a market leader.

After a diligent search process, we discovered that an Asian biotech company had advanced a product candidate in phase 3 clinical trials in Europe. The potential for the product to benefit patients, if approved by US regulators, was substantial, and we had interest in pursuing it. I led a small team to negotiate with the Asian company to grant us rights to the product to further develop and commercialize in return for an upfront payment and splitting a portion of the sales.

We spent about four months negotiating over the phone and in our offices in New Jersey. After considerable back and forth, we had agreed on the key financial terms and were finalizing some details when the Asian company invited us to their offices in Osaka to finalize the deal. The key financials were already agreed to, and, aside from some details regarding governance and how the companies would work together, we were close to signature. So I felt that a trip to Osaka could further the relationship and allow for an efficient end to the negotiations.

I took a small team, a total of three of us, to Osaka. After formalities, we began to discuss the deal. It quickly became clear that what we had previously agreed upon was no longer on the table. This was quite frustrating and risked the viability of the eye therapeutic business and even the jobs of the people who joined me on the trip. Emotions were running high, and what had originally been thought of as a straightforward exercise to close the deal became a nightmare.

While we needed to in-license the product to be successful as a business unit, beginning a partnership with a company that was changing previously agreed positions would likely lead to further disappointment and frustration in the future. We needed a foundation of trust if we were ever going to successfully collaborate and needed to send this message to our potential partners. How to communicate this effectively, without being disrespectful, would prove important if we were to salvage the deal.

I asked the Asian group, "We need to have a private room to discuss the current state of negotiations for a few minutes. Would that be possible?"

"Of course," they respectfully answered.

We then walked into a separate room. I started by saying, "I am quite surprised by what is happening and wanted to first confirm with both of you our common understanding. Robert, would you start by summarizing your viewpoint?"

Robert was obviously quite frustrated and simply blurted out, "They have gone back to a negotiating position that they had a month ago. It is pure bad faith negotiations—plain and simple." Mark forcefully nodded his head, so it was clear that the summary from Robert was the universal understanding.

I said, "Thanks, Robert. So we are all of the same opinion, before we talk about our response, let me remind you of our assessment of the opportunity, which was transformational for our franchise, and what we had originally assumed would get the deal done, which we are still below."

I paused to ensure that Robert and Mark had time to reflect on our situation.

I asked them for their thoughts in regard to our next move, which ranged from just continuing to negotiate the deal using the new deal terms to threatening to publicly disparage the reputation of the Asian negotiators.

After a further pause in the discussion, I decided, "While the deal terms are still good and the opportunity would be great, we cannot accept such behavior from a potential partner. We need to be able to trust each other as any relationship will have its challenges down the road. I am going to make the Executive Vice President of our company aware of our decision as it is high stakes."

Amazingly, I was able to get directly in touch with our EVP. I explained the situation: "We are prepared to walk, and I just want to be sure I have your support."

The senior executive, who is a tremendous leader and someone whom I greatly admired, responded briefly, "You have my full support. Let me know if there is anything I can do to help."

After the call, I went back to Robert and Mark and said, "We have full management alignment. Let me call them on this behavior and see if we can reset the relationship."

My colleagues seemed to agree with the approach, and we rejoined our counterparts from the other company.

I announced, "Thank you for the use of the private room. We have decided that it is best for us to leave as we feel that we are no longer discussing the agreed upon terms, but terms that we did not agree to several weeks ago. We need our partnership to be one that both parties are proud of and that is not the case right now." With that there was complete silence, and I motioned to Robert and Mark that we should begin collecting our bags to head back to the airport.

The Asian team quickly understood our seriousness because we had acted in a consistent manner and been true to our word in past dealings. They did not argue with us about our decision and huddled together quickly with significant concern in their eyes. When their huddle broke a few minutes later, their leader said, "Please hold on changing any of your travel plans and make yourself comfortable. There must be some misunderstanding. We would like to speak privately with our CEO. Please grant us thirty minutes and we will come back to you."

I accepted their request. We still needed to firm our return flights, and perhaps meeting with their CEO could lead to a positive resolution.

After what was closer to forty-five minutes, they came back. Their leader said, "Our CEO wishes to extend his greetings to you. We discussed the current situation, and he agreed that there must have been some misunderstanding. We wish to continue discussions with you based on our email of last week, and if there are any additional problems, our CEO has asked us to involve him as necessary. He expressed his personal commitment to being a great and trusted partner."

I said, "We are very appreciative of your CEO's involvement and commitment. Please let us gather briefly in the private room and come back to you." The three of us met briefly in the private room.

I spoke what was likely on everyone's mind. "From a purely business standpoint, it is clear that we should move forward and complete the deal, assuming no more misunderstandings. What are your thoughts concerning whether they will turn out to be a good partner?"

Mark jumped in first and said, "I can put clauses in the contract to ensure that we are protected."

I responded, "I have no doubt that you can, but that was not my question."

Robert chimed in with his insights, "I truly believe that this will reset the partnership. You showed that we will not put up with games and they understand that now. I don't think we will see that again."

I agreed with Robert and we came back to the joint room. I said "We are pleased that you clarified that this was a misunderstanding and that you do not anticipate any further misunderstandings. We trust the commitment of your CEO to be a trusted partner and would like to move forward as you described."

Whatever led them temporarily to switch their bargaining position was never clear to me, but they willingly returned to the trusted partner that we previously had known. They recognized that our decision was not a ploy because we had gained their trust through our interactions. We subsequently closed the deal terms within the next two hours and executed the agreement in a few weeks. We enjoyed a strong partnership with them after that and never had a similar problem.

The Seven Defining Traits

Trustworthy people come in all shapes and sizes, and no group of people owns this trait. Despite its many forms, societies around the world agree that the trait of being trustworthy is highly desired.[35] Not surprisingly, people are more apt to want to associate and collaborate with trustworthy people because they appreciate the ability to depend on that person or company to deliver on what is discussed. As depicted in the Trustworthy Decision Matrix, if someone is trustworthy, they are already working in two quadrants within the matrix that support a "Go" decision, with or without conditions depending on the difficulty of the project.

Even for a difficult project, people with a trustworthy track record should be considered for new initiatives that require trust, and it is simply a matter of whether additional resources are needed and should be committed to support the person or company to confirm the new project's approval. Conversely, for the untrustworthy company or person, they should only be considered and trusted for easy projects that are of low risk. That is because being trustworthy is a critical variable in the Trustworthy Decision Matrix and should be within any personal or organizational decision-making process.

Just as it is possible to become more trustworthy over time, it is possible to move across quadrants in the Trustworthy Decision Matrix. In the story concerning our Asian partner, we initially were conservative in assigning them a modest trust score and so took the lead role in areas of high complexity and in which they did not have clear experience. As we developed the relationship further and gained more trust in their abilities to exceed expectations, we thought of them as being able to share in difficult joint projects with the necessary support from our organization. Evaluating whether someone is trustworthy should not be a one-and-done process.

Despite its universal importance, there are no definitive scales or universally accepted measures of trustworthiness. Before trusting someone, we evaluate either consciously or subconsciously if they are trustworthy using our own experiences and intuition as a guide. Based on literature and my own experiences, I believe these are the seven defining traits of most trustworthy individuals:

- ► Reliability
- ► Integrity
- ► Honesty
- ► Respectfulness
- ► Responsibility
- ► Empathy and caring
- ► Being prone to guilt

Many of these traits are interrelated, so trustworthy individuals will typically behave consistently across all of them. While consistency across traits is normally observed, a person may be appropriately viewed as trustworthy when acting with one set of people and not worthy of trust when interacting with another. This may be a conscious choice by the trustee perhaps due to previous negative interaction with the trustor or driven by bias they have with potential trustors, such as a bias to not act trustworthy in front of strangers.

Trustworthy people do what they say that they will do. They are the people who, once they commit to something, can be counted on to show up and contribute as needed. You can depend on them in a variety of situations as their reliability does not turn off whether in professional or social settings. These people are often the critical foundation that sustains many groups and organizations. While they are viewed as highly supportive, reliable people do not quickly commit to things that they do not understand or believe in.

People who are trustworthy are consistent in their actions and values. They have the confidence to not pretend to be something they are not. They follow their own beliefs even when difficult, which are typically aligned with established moral principles.

Charles Marshall perhaps said it best: "Integrity is doing the right thing even when no one is watching."[36] We may not always agree on what is the right thing, and instead we place the greatest emphasis on the person to "walk the talk" versus being hypocritical or corrupt. Consistency of action and thoughts make someone trustworthy, not whether that person is popular or a good speaker.

Trustworthy people are honest. One of the quickest ways to lose trust is to lie or mislead others as it casts doubt on your motivations in relationships, whether new or mature. People appreciate that the truth is not always black or white, yet they have no patience for word games or other tactics that allow you to mislead without technically not telling the truth.

Increasingly, being transparent is also associated with honesty, although this is much more context dependent. For example, you may not mention the specific details of a friend's illness out of respect for their privacy or due to the inability of others to comprehend and still be viewed as honest. You also may not tell your staff that the company is assessing new organizational designs, sparing your team the inevitable anxiety and disruption that it will cause despite no recommendations even being made. Honest people are careful not to deceive people, and truthfulness is often viewed as a core component of integrity.

Honesty, like the other traits of trustworthiness, is not normally absolute in an individual. People are more likely to be honest with those they perceive as socially close, such as friends and family, compared to those they feel distant to, like strangers or acquaintances. This is because the perceived consequences of dishonesty are often lower when there is less emotional connection or accountability involved. This partially explains why a person may be highly trustworthy to one group of people and highly untrustworthy to another. These extremes are not typical within one individual as there is some consistency in natural tendencies over the long term—we are who we are—yet striking inconsistencies are possible in the short term within certain situations and different audiences.[37]

People who resort to humiliation or intimidation of others are hard to trust, unless you are of the same mindset or prejudice against a certain group of people. This lack of respect for others sends a message that the person does not care about the thoughts or interests of the other party.

Trustworthy individuals respect others and maintain good manners and values because they have an interest in some shared goal or effort, at least in the short term.

People who are trustworthy take responsibility for their actions and are accountable for their mistakes. They are willing to admit errors and work toward correcting them. It has been increasingly difficult for public leaders to make such apologies as it is often seen as a sign of weakness. Some political officials and celebrities have even helped establish the norm of "non-apology apologies," which focus on public reaction as opposed to the wrongdoing itself. Despite the popularity of these insincere apologies, people who take responsibility for their actions are more likely to be trusted by their peers.[38]

Trustworthy individuals show genuine concern and care for others. They tend to be supportive and nurturing in their relationships. In valuing the feelings of others, they wish to act in a way that builds trust and generates a positive environment. When someone perceives that another is concerned about their welfare, a feeling of trust is more likely to be sustained. While it was a red flag decades ago for a leader to show emotion, it has become increasingly accepted to build human connection and valued if authentic. These prosocial behaviors not only demonstrate trustworthiness, they also are often reciprocated once mutual trust is established.

Perhaps less obvious, the way a person experiences guilt has an important impact on how trustworthy they may be. A person's tendency to anticipate feeling guilty, termed guilt-prone, is the most defining attribute to being trustworthy, according to research conducted at the University of Chicago Booth School of Business. The researchers found that people who are high in guilt-proneness anticipate feeling guilty for committing a transgression and therefore avoid transgressing in the first place.[39] It's the impulse pulling at you to not do something that you will regret afterward.

In reaching this conclusion, these researchers conducted several experiments, one in which participants played an economic game. One player would receive money that they could pass on to a second player—and if they do, the money multiplies, and the second player has the choice of returning half of the spoils back to the first. In this particular study, the first player always passed along the money. Observing how the second player responded to this display of trust was the focus of the research.

Study participants who scored higher in measures of guilt-proneness, as determined by a questionnaire, chose to give back half of their money more often than people who had average levels of guilt. The most guilt-prone people were 1.6 times more likely to return the money than those whose scores fell in the middle. The researchers summarized that the people who were more guilt-prone were more trustworthy. They also found that guilt-proneness tended to be the best predictor of trustworthy behavior.[40]

Do these traits play out across personal, professional, and social settings? While the settings and context may cause subtle differences, the same traits that cause a person to be trustworthy in business will also result in a trusting relationship for friendships and beyond. Please keep in mind that although trust is critical in these situations, being trustworthy is not the only consideration. For example, a person will not typically buy a house if they do not like it, even though they may trust every party involved in the transaction. However, when asked about the most important quality in a real estate agent, survey respondents overwhelmingly cited trustworthiness and honesty as the top attributes.[41]

The Bottom Line

The traits of trustworthy people are common across personal, professional and social settings. The core traits include reliability, integrity, honesty, respectfulness, responsibility, empathy and caring, and being prone to guilt. Consistently demonstrating these traits across situations will help you to be trusted by friends, partners, and within organizations.

While trustworthy individuals tend to act consistently within most contexts, a person may be appropriately viewed as trustworthy when acting with one set of people and not worthy of trust when interacting with another, depending on many factors including the familiarity and relationship of the trustee with the trustor. Across almost all settings, demonstrating trustworthiness will lead to greater collaboration and positive decisions, as seen within the Trustworthy Decision Matrix, which specifically provides the framework for leveraging trust as the key decision variable for project approval and resource decisions.

The So What

Do you need to be concerned if you notice someone not demonstrating strength across one of the seven attributes that align with being trustworthy? There is no magic number for how many of the behavioral attributes you need to miss to cause you to move from being trustworthy to untrustworthy, yet they are so correlated with each other, weakness in one attribute is likely being also expressed in another that you may not have observed. Failure on any one of these attributes may create doubt as to whether the person is trustworthy, leading others to respond with caution, skepticism, or withdrawal.

Despite the significant downside of losing trust in someone, you should not be overly concerned if there is one instance that seems out of character, for there could be legitimate reasons, such as you misinterpreted what occurred, or the person was acting on different information than you have, maybe the person simply made a one-time mistake, or the situation forced a compromise among multiple groups. Even with these legitimate excuses, it should not stop you from questioning the person, especially if the issue was important to you, such as when you or your team are dependent on their deliverables, as talking through the issue may help you reassess the situation, and also the awareness may improve the performance of the other person.

Certainly, if a trend has begun to form—let's say that the person has missed two milestones on a project without offering an explanation— you need to speak up to ensure awareness of the missed expectation, alignment on corrective actions, and provide additional support as warranted. As seen in the research, when the person does not exhibit any responsibility or guilt for the situation being reviewed, they may be less trustworthy than you had originally thought. The only chance you have to reverse this trend is by communicating directly and clearly regarding the desired behavior and your observations. This may solve the issue, at least for the short term, and require monitoring to minimize the risk as part of a long-term plan.

Some people believe that it does not matter how a person behaves because, at the end of the day, if you hold the keys, no one gets through the door without your help. In other words, if a person is critical to some effort, people will overlook their misgivings and still work with them. We see this in many public and private arenas, whether it is an influencer who has a huge following, a person with significant political access and power, or even a business leader heading a large organization, as even when they run afoul of societal norms, people still work with them to get things done.

This rings especially true when alternative options are limited, which is often the case in the short term. The reasons are primarily twofold: (1) changing course highlights the original misstep in selecting the business leader or partner and forces conflict to the surface, and (2) moving on from the untrustworthy leader or ending the partnership may inflict significant damage on the shared resources or valuable pursuits that drove the collaboration in the first place. While continuing to work with an untrustworthy individual to avoid embarrassment or conflict is simply poor leadership, it is rational to continue working with such a person to minimize significant disruption in the short term.

For example, how many millions of dollars were lost to Bernie Madoff because people wanted to believe in his unrealistic investment returns and convoluted schemes? All the signs of fraud were there, yet hubris and embarrassment, even by informed experts, kept it quiet for far too long. There was no reason to continue such an untrustworthy relationship, and actually the longer that you stayed involved, the less likely you were to get back your original investment.

In contrast, let's look at a situation in which you have a leader of one of the most critical manufacturing processes. While she is an expert in this field and works hard when present, her track record for absenteeism is causing the company unusually high product rejections, and productivity is far from optimized. Yet no one has her skill level in the company or exists for competitors given the customized plant design and application. To simply fire her would essentially stop your ability to produce goods for a few months. As a result, you may have to live with that untrustworthy leader for much longer than you would want.

In most situations, especially given time, you should be able to switch out that business leader or, perhaps more likely, reduce your dependency on the expected deliverables from that collaborative effort. Even better, you could find an alternative to the problem individual and use that leverage to either enforce the necessary changes in the original partner or simply move over time to the preferred alternative. One exception: It is not so easy when that untrustworthy person is your boss or organizational leader.

Confronting an untrustworthy boss inherently has risks, but sometimes the person is just not aware of their behavior and may improve, at least incrementally, as requested, especially if you are an important member of their team. As I discussed previously, the ability to trust and trustworthy behaviors are developed early in life, so changing such ingrained behavior takes concerted effort beyond awareness. Expectations should be realistic—moving from untrustworthy to trustworthy does not happen often and certainly not overnight.

Speaking directly to your leader is a preferred approach instead of trying to convince your boss's superiors or the organizational senior management of the failings of your manager. After making your boss directly aware of your concerns, going to higher management or human resources is a much more palatable sequence. Unless a criminal act has taken place, a change rarely occurs through this route and not without significant time and effort. Given these realities, it is not surprising that good employees often resort to transferring to another role in the organization or finding a new organization to work for, if possible.

Winning Moves

Demonstrate trustworthy behaviors if you wish to build trust, close deals, and deliver exceptional performance.

- ► Remember that being trustworthy is not just about you but also caring about others.
- ► Don't assume that people are aware of their own behavior flaws and give them a chance to correct by calling attention to it in an appropriate way.
- ► Be wary of aligning yourself with individuals or organizations that are not consistently acting trustworthy.
- ► Keep a list of trustworthy behaviors with you and periodically assess your performance on these traits.

6

HOW TO BUILD SUSTAINABLE RELATIONSHIPS

W HEN I WAS LEADING ALL MARKETING efforts for in-licensing products at a major pharmaceutical company, we had determined strong interest in an innovative compound that was being developed to treat insomnia. Due to its potential to be effective yet not addictive, there was significant interest from other companies as well. As a result, we needed to approach the originator, a company in Denmark, with a strong, differentiated pitch that would elevate our interest above our competitors. This pitch would prove important to winning the deal because the financial assessments across companies would likely result in similar monetary terms.

In assembling a team to make such a pitch, I invited a young manager who was an expert in the science of sleep, but not an experienced presenter, to deliver some of our key arguments. I had worked with her on a separate internal project and found her to be insightful, hard-working, and full of management potential. She was excited to be involved because she rarely had opportunities to be in front of senior management, especially not with so much on the line.

While she had presented many times in the past, she typically came across as brutally factual, without some of the polish and softer skills that engage audiences. I spent a fair amount of time refining her presentation and coaching her on her talking points to ensure that she was confident and poised for success. She responded well to the feedback and refined her presentation to be clear and compelling. After several weeks, we headed to meet with the other company in Copenhagen and were hopeful of getting to the next steps.

I made the opening remarks and necessary introductions to get everyone comfortable at the start of the meeting, and the meeting was proceeding well. Unfortunately, a lightning storm was active during our meeting and the electricity was knocked out for at least the immediate area. Given that it was early afternoon, there was not a need for flashlights or significant safety concerns.

Still, several people from the other company reacted, "I guess you should work on getting back to the airport. No sense to waste your time without power."

Even people from my own company responded, "Sounds good. We'll reconnect virtually sometime soon." They could not envision us continuing the meeting because the presentation equipment was out of service.

I thought this was a missed opportunity and, with a key leader named Lars from the other company, convinced everyone that we could still continue with the meeting given that much of the conversation did not require electronics. "As long as we don't have a safety concern, let's keep going because we came a long way to be with you and the afternoon light is more than enough."

Someone from the other company asked, "What about the presentations? How can we really go through the material?"

"This next agenda topic is not data driven, so we can work without slides. I'll discuss with Lars how best to cover the subsequent topics," I responded.

We picked up from where we had left the conversation with the approximately twenty people in the meeting reengaged, although many were distracted.

We were approaching the point in the meeting for the marketing presentation. The manager I had been coaching was notably nervous, and I knew she felt uncomfortable not having slides to prompt her talking points. I recognized the situation and did not want to step in for her as I knew that this was her big moment.

I separately pulled Lars aside to talk through some ideas to maximize the remaining time together. I asked him, "How many people are key decision-makers on your side?"

Lars took some time to look at his company's attendees and then replied, "We really need four of our executives involved in any decision in this field."

I was relieved that it was not all ten who were present. I suggested, "That's great. We can have the four huddle by the battery-operated computer of our presenter so that they can see the slides. Everyone else can sit or stand a little farther away. Will that work for your company?"

"I am not sure, but let's try," said Lars.

I then went over to the manager who was to present the marketing slides and said, "I know this is not what we had planned, but I was able to get Lars to agree on a way that you can still present from your slides. Their most important people will simply look over your shoulders to view the presentation, and you can present as if there was no power outage. You will do great."

She really did not reply, but simply gave a nervous smile and a thumbs-up.

Given the unique environment, the attendees were quite engaged and the interest in the presentation was extremely high. To her credit, the manager made a great presentation, which left a strong impression on all attendees. We ended the meeting by exchanging commitments for next steps and enthusiastically shaking each other's hands. This potential disaster turned into an event that bonded us in ways that a normal meeting could not.

After concluding the meeting, we were well positioned to be viewed as a highly desirable partner, clearly meeting or exceeding our objectives. We needed to negotiate with the other party for a few months to reach a mutually agreeable deal and ultimately won the right to in-license the product in a competitive situation. The other company referred to the meeting in which we were huddled by a computer many times during our discussions. It clearly made a big impression on them and conveyed a willingness to work together under the most unpredictable of situations.

Importantly, the manager who made the key marketing presentations developed a new sense of confidence from the experience. Part of the reason was due to the trust that I showed in her to deliver the presentation, despite the stakes involved and how easy it would have been to do the talk myself. Like many situations, the greatest test for trust is when under pressure and that is when trust can become rock solid or broken overnight. As a result of her tremendous abilities and newfound confidence, she went on to have an exceedingly successful career.

The Trust Blueprint

The characteristics that make someone trustworthy can be transformed into key strategies for developing trust in relationships and organizations. The most critical behaviors for developing trust are to be consistent and reliable. You need to follow through on your commitments and do what you say you will do. This is clearly depicted within the Trustworthy Decision Matrix as a key driver for trusting someone or an organization on any new effort. Consistency of behavior builds credibility over time and creates a sense of psychological safety and security. When people know what to expect from others, it reduces anxiety and uncertainty and allows for more open and trusting interactions.[42]

In the story of the marketing manager, I clearly viewed her as worthy of taking on new efforts that were either new to her or difficult given her track record of success. Based on the Trustworthy Decision Matrix, she should not have been simply assigned the licensing project but supported with additional resources such as my direct involvement and coaching of her presentation. In using the matrix, it makes the decision an easy one and rewards trustworthy people with growth opportunities.

While consistency of strong results makes you a prioritized candidate for important projects, being consistent and reliable is not easy. Many times plans do not go as expected or something happens, such as a lightning storm knocking out power in a meeting, and it is hard to stick to the original commitments that were made. For example, you may miss a car payment because you decide to lend money to a friend or be late for a meeting due to heavy traffic. This can often be overlooked if you have established a track record of consistent and reliable behavior. Otherwise, regardless of the excuse, it provides a data point that creates doubt about your trustworthiness. Such data points can be the difference in a proposal being accepted or rejected as seen in the Trustworthy Decision Matrix.

Building and maintaining trust is an ongoing process that requires consistent, intentional actions and a commitment to open, mutually beneficial relationships. It requires you to practice honest and transparent communication whenever possible. Trustworthy people share information openly and candidly, even when it's difficult or uncomfortable. Just as important, you should avoid secrecy or withholding important updates, as this can quickly erode trust. While it is easier to communicate just what is happening, it is important to provide the reasons behind decisions and changes, so that others will not fill in the dots with false assumptions. Transparency about motives and processes reassures others of your integrity.

As I briefly mentioned in the previous chapter, there are times when being transparent is difficult for government or business leaders. For example, a business leader cannot disclose information to friends or family that would be non-public information and could lead to insider trading. In this case, transparency is communicating that you cannot disclose information on that subject due to company confidentiality provisions. Not only are you being transparent and honest in such circumstances but showing integrity, which could translate into the other person feeling that you can be trusted even without full disclosure.

Part of being honest is to be authentic. People become more authentic when they have strong self-awareness, which means they know what they value, their strengths and weaknesses, and how they are perceived by others. Communication stemming from authenticity comes across naturally and encourages genuine connection. Maintaining a facade of perfection or pretending to be interested in a political cause that you are not are examples of behaviors that are not genuine and have the potential to undermine trust in individuals when uncovered. People, especially leaders, need to be comfortable being themselves, including showing some vulnerability, to come across authentically.

In addition to giving communication, the trustworthy individual should listen actively and seek feedback. To build and maintain trust, you should make a habit of listening more than you speak. Encourage others to share their thoughts, concerns, and ideas, and show that you genuinely value their input. You need to regularly ask for feedback and, crucially, act on it. When people see their feedback leads to positive changes, their trust in you deepens. In contrast, if someone gives feedback that is ignored or not addressed, trust is decreased.

Trustworthy people are accountable for their actions. They make decisions aligned with their stated values and ethical standards, even when it's not easy to do so. This practice reinforces consistency and predictability, which are important for building trust. They admit mistakes promptly, take responsibility, and outline steps to make amends or improve. Trustworthy people avoid blaming others, although they will not shy away from criticism of individuals or systems that are impacting relationships or organizational performance. The trust they have built within those relationships or organizations allows people to understand that such comments are meant for improvement versus simply assigning responsibility for a mistake.

To build trust among project teams, plans or efforts need to be set with clear, realistic expectations for those involved, their responsibilities, and desired outcomes. It is not sufficient that the project leader feels good about the plan, but they must take the time to ensure everyone understands what is expected and how success will be measured.[43] A lack of common understanding among the project team can turn a project that was viewed as easy to become a difficult task to meet expectations. One of the more common ways projects fail, and trust is lost even before even starting the effort, is when the project leader overpromises the results to management or the project sponsor. This basic mistake sets the team up for failure, and the team loses trust in their leader as a result.

Very few projects go exactly as planned. When resources or circumstances change, the leader of the effort needs to communicate promptly and ensure everyone is aligned. Consistency in communication is fundamental to building and maintaining trust. If a mistake was made, it should not be overlooked but acknowledged along with the corrective action that is now required. Hiding important details or sugar-coating key issues can result in a lack of trust in subsequent communications.

In addition, the leader or project sponsor should be willing to reassess the underlying assumptions that supported moving forward with the project at key points during its implementation. Due to mistakes or new information that contradicts previous assumptions concerning a project that is ongoing, you should reevaluate trusting the leader or team to move forward using the Trustworthy Decision Matrix and this new information.

While many people find it quite challenging to reverse a decision in which personnel or other resource costs have already been committed, sometimes the best decision is to modify or stop projects to not waste resources further. The matrix can help frame the decision by incorporating changes in the trustworthiness of the people involved or the degree of its difficulty. The converse is also true for efforts that have greatly exceeded initial expectations; a reevaluation may support more funding and allow for even greater returns.

Whether during challenging times or opportunities for growth, a powerful way to become trusted in an organization is to be willing to trust others as well, treating trust as a precious resource that is not unattainable. Using a tool like the Trustworthy Decision Matrix can facilitate a thoughtful process in trusting others that standardizes the decision-making and is less prone to subjectivity. It is critical to limit any skepticism of your trust decisions by meeting the challenge directly with sound arguments and logic, as this can affect whether others have trust in you. Having a relationship in which both parties are trusted further solidifies the relationship and enables it to grow beyond its current base. However, you must avoid extending trust to others just on hearsay as this may lead to great disappointment and failure unless the other person merits such trust.

As in the story in Copenhagen, trust can be nurtured only by involving both parties in the decision-making. When I worked with Lars to solve for whether or not to continue the meeting, it was not one company dictating to the other. Instead, it was an open discussion in which each party's perspective was valued and a mutual objective, having a meaningful exchange of ideas, was achieved.

The Bottom Line

Developing trust takes time and consistent effort, but a few key practices not only help develop trust but also sustain it. These practices include being consistent and reliable, communicating honestly and transparently, listening actively and seeking feedback, being accountable for actions, setting realistic expectations, and extending trust to others. These practices can help build strong, trusting relationships over time. The most important factor is to demonstrate trustworthiness through your actions consistently, day after day.

The So What

As I have already shown, trust determines how quickly teams move, how openly they communicate, and how much effort they give beyond the minimum. Managers who intentionally build trust unlock commitment, creativity, and accountability that rules and incentives alone are unlikely to replicate. Trust is like mom and apple pie—everyone wants to be trusted or work for someone who is trustworthy.

Yet, if you have a track record of being a good leader, do you really need to spend all the time and effort to focus on developing and maintaining trust? Just like when you obtained your driver's license, even though you are certified as a good driver, you still need to obey the speed limit and practice safe driving habits. The beauty of being a good leader likely means that you are already performing in ways that develop and maintain a trustworthy environment. If so, do you really need to monitor and periodically reassess the trust people have in you?

The reality is that most of us are developing and adjusting to new situations and environments all the time, and we can rarely remain on cruise control and continue to be perceived as a good leader. For example, a leader may have exceeded all his organization's expectations for the five years prior to the COVID-19 pandemic, but are they necessarily a good leader now that their staff works in hybrid arrangements or remotely?

Or how about when they are promoted to manage the marketing of a product launch and had previously only led a support organization? It is also rare that you work with the same people year after year. As a result, leaders need to continually refine their skills to ensure they are creating a trustworthy environment for their organization.

What about the situation in which a leader knows they have only six months before being promoted to another area and have been asked to reduce staff by 20% before they move on? Building and maintaining trust may seem like a non-essential luxury as layoffs are always a lot of work and the extra sensitivity and transparency to maintain an environment of trust will just make things harder to execute. The exact opposite is true, especially in these situations of high uncertainty and change. That's where trust matters the most.

Consider how much easier it is to maintain a trustworthy environment than to build one from a starting point of mistrust. Without trust, people spend productive time by protecting themselves, and communication is guarded. Employees feel threatened and are less likely to buy in to whatever their management is selling. It may take years of consistent actions and care to overcome this skepticism, which unfortunately feeds on itself and infects even new or transferred employees. For the manager who thinks that they should not care because it will no longer be their problem, think again. Reputations travel quickly, and once branded as untrustworthy, it is difficult to be viewed differently.

It really comes down to the understanding that trust is a strategic multiplier that improves the likelihood of success for any short-term or long-term effort. With such understanding, a leader would not rationally make a tradeoff in effort that detracts from developing and maintaining trust. In fact, developing and maintaining trust should be one of the highest priorities for effective leadership of teams because of its impact on completing the current project and the increased likelihood of success in completing the next project.

Even though developing and maintaining trust is of critical importance, that does not make it any easier to execute. Far more organizations fail than succeed in doing so, partly because it is so much easier to lose trust than to gain it. People don't give trust automatically; they accumulate it through repeated experiences of trustworthy behavior, primarily reliability, honesty, and care. As a result, gaining trust is gradual—earned one behavior at a time.

However, trust can be lost instantly because it breaks expectations. When a leader violates trust—even when unintentionally—it triggers a sense of betrayal or uncertainty. So a single act of dishonesty, broken promise, or missed deadline can outweigh hundreds of trustworthy actions that came before. That is why you can never sleep on efforts to develop and maintain trust in their organization.

For new managers or leaders, the skills to develop and maintain trust may be tested early and often by their team. Organizations cannot just assume they will succeed and need to make a concerted effort to provide their teams with the tools to succeed. Using the Trustworthy Decision Matrix will lead to a similar conclusion for those new managers and leaders who have a track record of meeting expectations in their previous roles. Some well-tested support practices include mentoring them by others in the organization who are proficient at developing and maintaining trust and providing training, as available. These tools will likely pay immediate dividends and also reinforce the commitment of trust throughout the organization.

Winning Moves

Make building and maintaining trust a focus throughout a professional relationship.

- ► Avoid actions that break commitments or create doubt as to your reliability.
- ► Be realistic in planning group efforts and seek buy-in from those involved.
- ► As mistakes happen, first assess your contributions and be wary of blaming others.

- ► Communicate authentically for understanding.
- ► Ensure that you are listening at least as much as you are talking.
- ► Be willing to trust others who are trustworthy.
- ► Provide new leaders with tools to succeed in building and maintaining trust.

7

REPAIRING WHAT MATTERS MOST

THE SALES TEAM IN THE BOSTON district of my life sciences company had lost all trust in their sales manager. Let's just say there were ethical and business reasons why he was no longer there.

I was asked to take over and lead the team. Now that sounds challenging in the best of circumstances. But this wasn't the best of times at all. Even worse, I had never been in a sales force during my professional career, yet I knew it was a valuable skill and experience. I was quite honored and excited. I'm not sure the team felt the same way.

While I was confident that I could leverage my adjacent skills and I could quickly learn new ones to succeed, the existing team of sixteen professionals, ranging from the newly hired to salespeople with over fifteen years of experience, likely felt that the situation in their world had hit rock bottom. Each sales representative had a defined sales geography and product responsibility, with significant overlap, so trust in each other and coordination was essential to individual and team success. It was obvious that this group was mostly operating at an individual level, although intuitively I knew (and they knew) this situation was on life support.

The level of trust in each other and the company was lower than low, and many of the salespeople probably considered leaving the company to go to competitors. Their previous leader had done a poor job in negotiating sales and performance objectives, so it was virtually impossible for them to hit their sales bonuses. He was also unable or unwilling to provide the guidance and selling resources to help the team meet those objectives. Talk about coming in to coach during halftime with the team behind by double digits.

I needed to build an environment of trust, not only in respect to me but also to repair trust in the company if we were to retain these skilled professionals and meet expectations.

One of the first tasks I did was to meet with the sales force as a group and introduce myself with the transparency of my background, not having sales experience, but other skills that could elevate their efforts. I communicated, "I want to be upfront with you that I never have been in your shoes as a sales representative. That has its weaknesses but also strengths. I do not come with a bias as to the only way to promote our products or to engage with our customers. I also have a perspective and expertise that will complement yours and that over time you may find quite valuable and worth directly incorporating in your planning and execution. I simply ask that you be open to the possibilities and whatever we do, we put the customer and doing the right thing as our priorities."

I also communicated what I could about the past manager, acknowledging the disappointment that must have been caused, and I listened to their views about what happened and how it may have hurt them.

The silence in the room as I began to speak was uncomfortable, yet respectful. I ended my introduction with an invitation to hear what was on their minds.

After everyone had a chance to speak if they desired, I declared, "Thanks everyone for the transparency and insights shared today. I know it was not easy to do and what you endured was quite disappointing. I really need you to turn the page and give me a chance to gain your trust and rebuild an environment in which we will thrive together and feel good about it along the way."

I then reiterated our common objectives and stated that, instead of addressing administrative tasks for a full day each week as was common, I would absorb that time during my nights and spend the entire month with them on visits with their customers and targeted customer events.

When asked what time we would start, I asked them what time they typically started. They told me that the previous manager usually met with them at noon and left late in the afternoon. I restated the question by asking them when they started the workday, and we agreed to meet each day at 8:00 a.m. and ended whenever the last customer appointment was, usually into the evening. By consistently showing up on time and being prepared to make the most of our time together, I started to gain their trust. When I moved from not just observing but using insights that I gained from my experiences at the company headquarters to help the sales representatives to address customer questions, we began repairing the damaged trust relationship.

By the end of the first month, I had been on so many customer calls across the sixteen different sales styles that we had on the team, I could point to some best practices and began truly helping the sales team share those practices and consider new ways of collaboration. I also tried to make the time to listen to them, find out who they were, what they wanted to achieve, and address any obstacles that we needed to solve to accomplish those goals.

If I could not address a request, I would explain why, quickly and transparently. When I was able to help them, such as providing better information on advertising programs being sent on by headquarters, it was well received. I also had the sales representatives meet as a team once a month to improve the connected points they had, sharing challenges and successes, and extending an environment of trust beyond my direct involvement.

While there were many additional steps along the way to creating a trustworthy relationship for the team and rebuilding trust in the company, it is worth summarizing that we achieved the highest performance versus objectives in our region during our first full year together, and I was awarded the sales manager of the year for the Northeast. It is an understatement to say that it was only possible through the trust we had established in each other. That trust needed to be nurtured each day as repairing trust takes focus and consistent effort.

Course Correction

Broken trust can tear any relationship apart. While some people believe that time heals all wounds, it still takes considerable effort and thoughtful approaches. Repairing trust is one of the most challenging yet crucial tasks we may face in our personal and professional relationships. When trust is broken, the impact can be profound, often leading to feelings of betrayal, anger, and disappointment.

In personal settings, the repercussions can cause long-lasting grudges, separation, and depression. As Friedrich Nietzsche said, "I'm not upset that you lied to me, I'm upset that from now on I can't believe you."[44] In professional settings, broken trust can result in decreased productivity, low morale, and high turnover. In society, broken trust can lead to unrest and instability. For business, mistrust can devastate leading brands. Approximately 53% of consumers said they stopped purchasing from a brand after a loss of trust in the past year and 44% of consumers said they told friends and family about that loss of trust.[45] The damage can go far beyond a brand as well. It has been more than a decade since Volkswagen was found to have rigged emissions testing devices in their diesel vehicles to appear more environmentally safe than they were and their reputation still suffers from that scandal.[46]

Repairing trust is not just about mending what's broken; it's about creating a stronger foundation for the future. It's an opportunity to learn, grow, and build more resilient relationships. To repair trust, it's important to understand why it was broken in the first place. Was it due to miscommunication, unmet expectations, or a violation of values? Self-reflection before acting is important to be able to express your thoughts to others. Understanding the root cause will also help to prevent future breaches.

In order to begin repairing the damage, you cannot wait too long in self-reflection before addressing those affected. The first communication to others needs to acknowledge that trust has been broken. This requires honesty and humility. Whether the breach was intentional or accidental, recognizing its impact is crucial. When acknowledging the damage caused by the broken trust, it is important to take responsibility for actions or decisions that led to the loss of trust. This involves owning up to mistakes, admitting faults, and understanding the hurt caused.

Instead of just stating that you are sorry, the person needs to focus on their role for the apology to be sincere and genuine. A true apology goes beyond mere words and demonstrates a commitment to change. Characteristics for a good apology include being sincere, specific, and acknowledging the pain caused.[47] After the acknowledgment and apology, both parties would begin engaging in an honest dialogue about what went wrong, how it affected them, and what they need to feel secure moving forward. This may not happen immediately, but it is important for the closure of all individuals.

A classic example of a corporate apology done well occurred when Johnson & Johnson experienced supply issues with its line of o. b. tampons, which were abruptly taken off the shelves. The company sent a personalized apology, in the form of a song, to all 65,000 plus women in the company's database. To personalize the apology, the song contained the customer's name, if available. Many customers shared their videos on social media, which helped Johnson & Johnson regain the trust of their customers.[48]

While you may be able to avert a crisis, trust can only be rebuilt through consistent, trustworthy actions over time. It's about showing, not just telling, that you can be trusted again. Can a peer ever regain the trust of a coworker from whom they stole an idea? When and how can trust be rebuilt, if at all?

Not surprisingly, the same practices that lead to building trust are the focus of rebuilding trust. Consistency helps to gradually restore confidence. Keeping promises, no matter how small, is crucial in the process of rebuilding trust. When people see that commitments are honored, their faith in the relationship can slowly be restored. Being reliable and dependable in everyday interactions reinforces trust. It shows that you can be counted on, which is a critical aspect of trust.

Even when doing everything right, trust may not be repaired overnight. It takes time for wounds to heal and for trust to be restored. Patience is required from both parties, as the process may involve setbacks and challenges. You should try to rebuild trust incrementally, step by step. Each positive interaction contributes to the gradual restoration of trust. It's important to celebrate any small victories along the way.

One key advantage of a breach of trust is that it can prove to be a learning opportunity. You should reflect on what went wrong, what could have been done differently, and how the relationship can be strengthened moving forward by its correction. This process of repairing trust can lead to growth in the relationship. It can deepen the understanding between individuals, enhance empathy, and ultimately strengthen the bond between them.

While most actions need to be led by the one who made the breach, it is important for the affected person to communicate forgiveness in some authentic way if the trust relationship is to be reestablished. It doesn't mean forgetting what happened, but it does mean letting go of resentment and being willing to move forward. Holding onto grudges can prevent the restoration of trust and the healing process.[49]

Relationships that have gone through the process of repairing trust often emerge stronger. The experience can lead to deeper understanding, enhanced communication, and greater resilience. When future challenges arise, the relationship is better equipped to handle them because of the foundation of trust that has been rebuilt. It also has an important benefit in personal development as renewed confidence, based on your realization that trust can be restored, allows you to understand that relationships can survive and thrive even after setbacks. More than 86% of couples stay together when both partners agree to be vulnerable, completely honest, and dedicate themselves to the process of rebuilding trust after betrayal.[50]

The effectiveness of apologies has been studied across multiple disciplines, including psychology, communication, and business. Roy Lewicki and his colleagues conducted a study published in *Negotiation and Conflict Management Research* that tested different components of an apology.[51] They identified six elements that make an apology more effective:

- Expression of regret
- Explanation of what went wrong
- Acknowledgment of responsibility
- Declaration of repentance
- Offer of repair
- Request for forgiveness

They found that acknowledging responsibility was the most important factor, followed by offering to repair the situation. The more elements an apology included, the more likely it was to be accepted.

A study by Holley Hodgins and Elizabeth Liebeskind found that apologies perceived as sincere significantly increased the likelihood of forgiveness.[52] Sincerity was often judged by nonverbal cues (such as eye contact, tone of voice) and whether the apology matched the severity of the offense. Research by Alfred Allan and associates showed that forced apologies are less effective than voluntary ones, as they lack sincerity ("Tell your financial colleague that you're sorry that you lost the expense report.").[53] In this study, participants who received voluntary apologies were more likely to forgive than those who received forced or insincere apologies. While these studies are consistent with our intuition, the research validates the need to be both sincere and unforced.

Research by Steven Scher and John Darley demonstrated that timely apologies were perceived as more sincere and were more likely to be accepted.[54] Apologies made shortly after the offense were more effective compared to those delayed for a significant period. Studies suggest that for more severe offenses, a simple apology might not suffice. An experiment published in *Psychological Science* found that in serious ethical violations, people expect reparative actions along with an apology. The apology alone was insufficient for repairing trust.[55] Society seems to have embraced the need for companies to combine apologies with financial penalties. We have seen a steep increase in fines for ethical violations including when Wells Fargo had to pay $3 billion for falsifying bank accounts.[56]

Studies have shown that apologies can repair relationships by fostering forgiveness and rebuilding trust. In 2010, a meta-analysis led by Ryan Fehr reviewed 175 studies and found that apologies facilitate forgiveness and contribute to trust restoration, especially when combined with reparative actions. Specifically, apologies help reduce negative emotions like anger and resentment.[57] Research published in *Frontiers of Psychology* also found that when people received apologies after being wronged, they experienced a decrease in anger and were more willing to reconcile.[58]

Given how global our business collaborations are today, it is important to note regional differences in regard to apologies. A cross-cultural study by William Maddux and colleagues found that people from different cultures respond to apologies differently. In collectivist cultures, such as Japan, apologies focus more on maintaining group harmony and relationships and were often offered even for minor offenses. In individualist cultures, such as the US, apologies tend to emphasize individual responsibility and guilt.

Studies show that apologies from companies can help repair brand image, especially when they are accompanied by corrective actions.[59] Not surprisingly, when companies apologize for service failures and take action to correct the mistake (let's say they send refunds or do product recalls), customer satisfaction and loyalty increase significantly compared to offering only one or neither.[60] A study by Peter Kim and colleagues found apologies that were paired with a change in behavior or compensation were far more successful in rebuilding trust than those that only involved words.[61] Early in its life cycle, Apple did not want anything to slow the growth of its music streaming service, so it only took twenty-four hours to apologize and take action in changing its policy of not paying artist royalties after a complaint by Taylor Swift.[62]

Apologies done poorly can cause more harm. Studies confirm that apologies that don't accept responsibility or appear to shift blame can make the situation worse. Even when involved in legal proceedings, companies can still express empathy and regret for the impact of the situation. Being up front, even acknowledging that the company cannot comment further due to legal proceedings, demonstrates transparency and caring for those involved, without taking on unnecessary liability while the case is ongoing.

Researchers found that people are less likely to forgive when apologies are perceived as excuses or as downplaying the offense.[63] People still remember when British Petroleum (BP) chief executive Tony Hayward apologized for the Deepwater Horizon oil disaster and famously focused on himself when he complained that he "wanted his life back."[64]

More broadly than just apologies, rebuilding trust is challenging but possible. The process of rebuilding trust is complex and requires open communication, honesty, time, and consistent actions that show commitment to change and repair, as I did with the sales team. It typically involves discussing events in extensive detail, answering all questions, and maintaining transparency and vulnerability.

Not surprisingly, people with more prior relationship experience are more likely to trust again after a breach of trust compared to those with less experience. The emotional state of the betrayed person plays an important role in their ability to trust again. Betrayal can lead to a range of negative emotions, including disappointment, anger, and fear. If someone is tremendously hurt emotionally by the other person, it will take longer to repair the relationship and require more consistent trustworthy behaviors.[65]

The Bottom Line

Trust that is broken can ruin relationships. In many cases, the betrayal causes significant impact and emotions ranging from anger to disappointment. However, honest and concrete steps can repair and rebuild the relationship. This process usually starts with an apology, followed by consistent trust-building actions.

The effectiveness of apologies is well supported by empirical research. Studies show that apologies work best when they acknowledge responsibility, are sincere, timely, and backed by reparative actions. Conversely, insincere or poorly executed apologies can exacerbate the situation, highlighting the importance of delivering a thoughtful and genuine apology. While some relationships will never reach the same level of trust, the same actions that led to building the foundation of trust can be effective in repairing the damage.

The So What

Everyone hates to admit a mistake. It is so much easier to pretend no one noticed and just move on. Doesn't everyone make mistakes anyway?

Current practice by many celebrities and politicians is not to admit a mistake or apologize as that is seen as weakness. If circumstances force some comment to be made, a non-apology apology is delivered that is so vague, you often do not even know what the issue is. These public figures set the tone for the rest of us and make it harder for us to do what works best to repair and rebuild trust.

The evidence is overwhelming that apologies work. Apologies signal that integrity is more important than ego and build organizational accountability. When a leader models the way and admits a mistake, it reminds people that leaders are human as well—capable of empathy, reflection, and growth. That vulnerability makes leaders more relatable and approachable and thereby improving morale and engagement. Importantly, it reinforces a culture where people can feel safe admitting errors and learning from them. No organization that is looking to innovate, collaborate, or improve can thrive without accepting mistakes.

So when you make a mistake as a leader, don't view it as a scarlet letter or a call to rally your defenses. Think of the mistake as a teachable moment to model the values that you want for your organization or team, as odds are that someone else in your organization will make a mistake as well. This mindset can be just as important as the actions or apologies that follow to repair and restore trust.

One of the first steps in transforming an error into a learning moment is to make an apology. Clear best practices concerning the aspects and delivery of an apology based on empirical evidence are summarized earlier in this chapter. However, it is worth noting here that the same apology speech that works for one person will likely not work for another because, when trust is broken, people feel betrayed and are skeptical. They do not want an apology that can be interpreted as insincere or just checking a box; they want something genuine and real.

While a well-designed and executed apology is essential on the path to restoring and rebuilding trust, it is often overlooked that an apology is just the start. Does the leader follow through on what was said or just take a bow for admitting that they were human? The next steps will determine the credibility of the apology and likely the credibility of the person who delivered it. Sometimes more trust is lost after the apology than before.

The next steps don't need to be dramatic, but they must align with the substance of the apology. For instance, if a leader apologizes for speaking directly with a key customer without informing the responsible account team, the leader should meet with the team to clarify expectations and reinforce a protocol that prevents similar lapses. This protocol should be broadly shared across account teams to restore trust in the wider organization. In addition, the leader should collaborate with the affected account team to ensure their relationship with the customer remains strong—helping restore the team's standing and preventing the customer from bypassing them in future interactions.

Just as when developing and maintaining trust, restoring and rebuilding trust takes time, consistent actions, and needs to be a priority. It is shortsighted to simply deliver a great apology and have a few meetings as follow-up to think that the trust has been restored. Trust is too delicate and difficult to gain for that. Restoring and rebuilding trust must remain a high priority and area of focus throughout whatever time is necessary, depending on the damage that was originally done. When restoring trust is successful, the organization can become much stronger and resilient as a result of turning a mistake into a true learning opportunity.

The first step that I took when meeting with my new Boston sales team was to deliver a sincere apology and follow-up with concrete actions to restore and rebuild that trust. While my primary efforts were all about trust, the business turned around quickly as a direct result from those interventions. We went from a declining business to one of the fastest growing in the country and were able to sustain that performance while I was the sales leader. I cannot take credit for anything magical that I did in terms of sales strategy and believe that it was instead all about creating an environment of trust that supported talented individuals to drive exceptional performance.

Winning Moves

Treat key mistakes as opportunities to reinforce leadership values by acknowledging the misstep, taking accountability for it, and resolving with transparency and urgency.

- ► Regularly evaluate your organization or team for signs that trust may have been compromised.
- ► Acknowledge that trust has been damaged honestly, with humility and specificity.
- ► Offer an apology that emphasizes your role and the hurt you caused.
- ► Start rebuilding trust through reparative and corrective actions.
- ► Prioritize and resource as necessary the rebuilding of trust within the organization for as long as needed.
- ► Continue to evaluate the strength of relationships and do not only rely on self-observations.

8

THE LEADERSHIP EDGE

A CEO and founder of a twenty-person company with a market capitalization below $100 million had painstakingly nurtured the company's biggest asset through various clinical trials to get to the point of the last pivotal trial, with a price tag of around $50 million. For obvious reasons, I need to keep the details vague, but the point is the point.

As the ability to raise that kind of money for a small company without a proven track record was limited, they needed to partner or sell their asset. Given that challenging environment, I was brought in to lead a business development process for the company to maximize their returns for the asset and retain some strategic options such as retaining rights to market the product outside of the US.

This was not a new scenario for me as my consulting firm directly supports CEOs whose companies are at a pivotal reflection point in their life cycles, like this one. The CEO of this company was quite smart and driven, with a tremendous passion for his small team, and the fit and timing were almost ideal for me to come in and help the company. I often faced challenges in trust given the magnitude of the decisions these companies were making, even though that was the reason I was hired.

Over a few months, we reached out to many companies whom we thought might have interest in the product and eventually got to a point when there were about ten companies interested. We then gave deadlines for each company to submit their proposal and communicated that we would select up to three companies to negotiate with. The process worked extremely well as we had interested companies and bids submitted. We ultimately focused on one company, given the strategic fit and a compelling initial offer, to further negotiate with and try to consummate an out-licensing deal, leaving the others as backups.

As with many small biotech companies, the founders and senior scientists have often spent much of their adult life and career in pursuit of advancing one product. Given that any deal would result in their losing control of their professional baby, the internal company discussions were often emotional and not only about financial considerations.

While I was not told directly, the process I was running and my guidance were being shadowed at key milestones by an expert business development consultant and a banking friend of the CEO. This was not surprising given the stakes involved, and I was willing to undergo credible validation through the various decisions that needed to be made. I did not view the arrangement as second-guessing my guidance, but as a way to better ensure that we would arrive at the best deal value. By being professional and respectful of this arrangement, I gained significant trust and respect from the CEO in a short amount of time.

Once I started negotiating with the lead company and raised the deal value from $50 million to over $500 million, we needed to make a key decision in terms of an additional counteroffer for a remaining milestone. I put forth an argument to justify $200 million for this remaining milestone to be paid to the company if it were to be achieved—a milestone in which both parties would have exceeded expectations and enjoyed over $1 billion in profits. The business development consultant and banking executive both panned the idea as they felt it was a figure that they had never seen before and would surely insult the targeted partner.

I told the CEO, "I respectfully don't agree. We should not negotiate against ourselves and instead let's put forward a number that makes sense from our analysis. If the number is not acceptable, we almost always have the chance to come back with a lower value."

Still, the CEO was notably nervous about disrupting the negotiations. This was high stakes for the CEO, who cared so much for his people and the potential patients that would be served that he often could not sleep. I reminded the CEO of all the previous decisions that had gone well and the rationality for offering the $200 million if achieving that milestone. At the end of the day, it simply came down to trust.

The CEO came back to me in a few days and stated, "I do not know what the right decision is, but I trust you to make the right one."

As a result, we made the milestone counter proposal of $200 million, and it was accepted without much pushback from the other company. Even with that added milestone, the deal value was highly desirable for both parties, but most importantly from my perspective, it likely will enable this small company to blossom into the company they aspired to become. Like many things, it all came down to trust.

The Buck Stops Here

The imperative of trust is most critical to leaders, whether business, government, or other, as they cannot succeed without the buy-in of followers. Multiple support industries have emerged to help leaders build trust within their organizations. For instance, trust is widely recognized as a core component of leadership training. The global corporate leadership training market was valued at $33.9 billion in 2023 and is growing at a CAGR (Compound Annual Growth Rate) of 8.95%.[66] That is a lot of money being spent on a trait that we develop as a child and experience every day. Is there such a need?

There is no such need if you ask business executives. According to a study fielded by PwC (PricewaterhouseCoopers) in 2024, 86% of US business executives think employee trust is high. Unfortunately, in the same study, only 67% of the employees of those leaders say they highly trust their employer. It appears that business leaders do not have a good sense for evaluating trust within their organizations. The gap has only continued to widen in recent years.[67]

One reason that company leaders may be overly optimistic about trust levels is that they don't have internal structures in place to consistently identify where the trust expectation gap exists. Many companies say they measure trust, but those metrics are often subjective and don't fully capture the current sentiment across stakeholder groups such as employees, customers, and investors. These often include metrics such as customer satisfaction and employee engagement, which are related to trust but are only part of the picture when it comes to trust.[68] Companies that move beyond these partial measures can better identify where they should focus.

A valuable exercise for a business or organization to go through is to use the Trustworthy Decision Matrix in thinking about employee retention. How well does the organization consistently meet the needs of the employee, whether, for example, an average employee focusing on work and life balance or a high-performing employee concerned about advancement? If a company is not trusted, using the matrix, it falls in quadrants 3 or 4, which means that the employee would only trust the company for their employment if their job was easy or had little downside to working there. That does not sound like the employee profile for top talent and can leave the company at a great competitive disadvantage in terms of talent.

Executives may also misinterpret signals to overestimate the trust of their followers, reinforcing a bias that comes automatically with their position. Even though an employee may work hard or deliver the expected results, the employee does not necessarily need to trust their manager but could be performing in this manner due to their own personal integrity, drive, and responsibility. This may become an issue when something does not go to plan or urgency beyond the agreed expectations is needed. Trust is often required for someone to go beyond the accepted relationship and put themselves at some level of risk.

Despite the lack of awareness of organizational distrust, businesses feel its impact. When trust is low, businesses and individuals have to spend more time and resources on formal contracts, monitoring, and enforcement mechanisms.[69] Low trust can lead to inefficient practices like vertical integration, in which the company acquires functions instead of letting them operate independently, or reliance on long-term relational contracts, so that the parties are contractually bound in a relationship, even when other arrangements would be more cost-effective.[70] This increases the costs of doing business and makes partnerships more difficult to form and sustain.

The employee-related impacts have been studied in even more detail. Firms that are not trusted find their employees are less likely to invest, delegate responsibilities, or take risks on new ventures. Such practices inhibit productivity, creativity, and growth. Research by Paul Zak showed that highly trusted workplaces enjoy 50% higher employee productivity and 13% fewer sick days compared to low-trust environments.[71]

In the same study, employees reported 74% less stress, 106% more energy at work, 50% higher productivity, 13% fewer sick days, 76% more engagement, 29% more satisfaction in life, and 40% less burnout when in high-trust environments. Employees who don't trust their employers are more likely to leave and thereby increase recruitment and training costs.[72] With the challenges in recruiting and retaining top talent, these risks are quite significant and cannot be overlooked.

To make matters even more complex, remote work or telework has become a key component of the work force since the COVID-19 pandemic caused employers to adjust workplace operations for safety reasons. Many employers encouraged or required their employees to work remotely and, while several companies have reversed their positions on remote work, the share of workers who work remotely continues to grow. According to the US Bureau of Labor Statistics, 36 million people teleworked or worked at home for pay, which accounted for 23% of people at work in the first quarter of 2024, growing from 20% the prior year.[73]

How do you manage people with whom you do not have regular in-person contact? While the question remains a good one, it is far from new to management. Many departments of large organizations have operated this way for many years, most notably in sales, in which sales managers may go several weeks without catching up with their salespeople in person. Still, the breadth and scale of remote working has challenged management to come up with new ways to inform, motivate, coach, and monitor performance.

Remote work depends on trust between the manager and employee, and the Trustworthy Decision Matrix can help guide the assessment from both perspectives. Fully enabling remote work to be successful requires the company to establish predictable and consistent communication schedules and forums in order to connect people and specifically a manager with their employees to develop and sustain relationships and build trust through those interactions.[74] Given the challenge in evaluating remote work, considerable thought and effort needs to focus on implementing performance management programs where goals are clear and easily tracked. To the degree that productivity can be measured easily and objectively, the more likely trust will be facilitated.

Measuring productivity without careful thought can be counterproductive. A study by Chase Thiel and colleagues surveyed more than 100 employees across the US to find that monitored employees were substantially more likely to take unapproved breaks, disregard instructions, damage workplace property, steal office equipment, and purposefully work at a slow pace. A subsequent study by the same research team asked 200 employees to complete a series of tasks, letting half of them know that they would be working under electronic surveillance. The workers who knew they were being monitored were more likely to cheat than those who did not know whether they were being monitored.[75] This is consistent with the idea that when workers feel that they are not being trusted, they feel less likely to act trustfully with their employers.

While companies have performed relatively well managing trust in recent years, government institutions have lagged significantly. Trust in government remains low in many countries, including the United States. In the US, as of April 2024, according to a survey of 800 US adults by the Partnership for Public Service, only 23% of Americans say they trust the federal government to do what is right "just about always" (2%) or "most of the time" (21%).[76] Trust levels in most other countries are also below 50%.

The Organisation for Economic Co-operation and Development (OECD) conducted a survey for its thirty-eight member countries and found that around 39% of people had high or moderately high trust in their country's national government, while 44% had no or low trust.[77]

For governments that have created an environment of trust, the impact on its systems and citizens can be significant. Studies have found that a one standard deviation increase in trust is associated with a 0.7 standard deviation increase in judicial efficiency and a 0.3 standard deviation reduction in government corruption.[78] In more general terms, higher trust is associated with better working courts and less corruption. While intuitive and self-reinforcing, it is worth pointing out these facts as governments often struggle in these dimensions.

Not surprisingly, countries with higher levels of trust tend to experience higher rates of GDP growth. One of the reasons is that in more trusting societies, business exchanges tend to be more frequent. Due to not having an environment of high trust, disengagement was estimated to cost US companies approximately $450 billion to $550 billion annually.[79] Citizens who distrust firms can go beyond disengagement and demand stricter regulations, which can stifle business activity. For example, as a result of the 2008 financial crisis, citizens and advocacy groups demanded more protection from predatory lending by banks. The Consumer Financial Protection Bureau (CFPB) was formed under the Dodd-Frank Wall Street Reform and Consumer Protection Act, which created several new protections and oversight that financial firms consistently argued resulted in significant compliance costs and waste that did not benefit consumers.[80]

The Bottom Line

With the losses due to a low-trust business environment estimated to be at least $450 billion, it is safe to assume that leaders should be prioritizing creating and reinforcing trust within their respective organizations. It is not sufficient for leaders to simply implement better interpersonal skills as they need to create structural ways to monitor trust and feedback processes as well, among others, to assist in steering organizational trust. The disconnect between business leaders' perception of trust and their employees provides clear evidence of the need.

Especially for businesses and governments, trust acts as a lubricant for commercial effectiveness and employee interactions. When it breaks down, the resulting friction creates waste and lost opportunities in the affected organizations. Remote work further constrains trust-building interactions with employees, so additional focus needs to be given to trust-building activities such as predictable and consistent communication schedules with remote workers.

When efforts effectively transform the workplace to make employees feel that their organization is trustworthy, employees are more likely to stay with an organization and have higher productivity. Building and maintaining trust should therefore be seen as a high priority for the leadership of businesses and governments.

The So What

A leader of an organization or team needs to establish metrics to evaluate whether the group is achieving its objectives and is positioned for future success. The traditional metrics of income, profitability, growth, market share, and customer retention are no-brainers. Do you really need to add another metric about being trustworthy? Is a check-the-box objective like hosting a speaker over lunch once a year to give a brief talk about ways to be more trustworthy good enough? Of course not.

The answers to these questions should be obvious due to all the empirical data and evidence that have been previously presented on the importance of trust to a successful organization. Yes, you need to include trust in the internal measurement grid; otherwise, it will not be prioritized or serve as a leading indicator of organizational health. When trust is low, employees are less efficient because people are doing the minimum required and spending time and resources to cover themselves for any blame since they do not feel the company has their back. Perhaps worse, opportunities are not being captured due to the extra effort required and the lack of faith that the organization will reward them.

Putting trust on an internal performance grid offers managers important insights, usually months before a significant increase or decrease in performance, that will allow the leader to adjust practices to maximize company efficiency and output. One of the most important arguments to measuring trust is that a change in trust will eventually lead to a change in other metrics that are critical to the company. Getting ahead of problems to correct them or maximizing internal strengths and capabilities are what leaders do best.

Assuming that trust is put on an organizational grid, what should the goal be? In other words, should management target a "10" or an incremental change versus a time before? That question could just as easily relate to any other management target that is being set—measuring versus a standard outside of your organization or looking to improve from whatever score where you are currently.

While it is a good idea to have a clear absolute goal that you are shooting for, it makes a lot more sense to initially target improvement as the benchmarks are far from universally accepted, and it will be easier to establish short-term success and momentum by showing improvement than achieving an external benchmark.

Trust scores are operationalized through pulse surveys and analytics dashboards benchmarked against historical surveys or peers, if working with a consulting firm that has sufficient data. There are costs associated with administering the survey, answering the survey questions, assessing the survey results, and communicating the survey results, which are not trivial. However, the mere announcement that the organization is committing resources to measuring trust can meaningfully increase trust within the organization because it proves that the organization cares about trust. Like any effort that is initiated, when the follow-up is non-existent or flawed, any goodwill that was built will quickly disappear.

A bigger question that needs to be asked even before the measurement plan is agreed upon is what to do with the results. While you should expect some incremental bump from just announcing the organization cares about trust, there is no guarantee that the scores will be comparatively good versus a peer set or improve over a baseline after actions are taken. This risk of looking bad on trust is actually the reason for performing a survey and motivates real action to correct any issues.

Just as there are unknowns regarding other key organizational measures such as market share or sales, aligning the organization on trust scores moves the discussion out of the abstract and into practical reality.

If you agree that trust is a core driver of organizational efficiency and performance, you need to take action to measure it and monitor it in order to best manage trust.

Once measurement begins, you are more than halfway there. When the trust scores are strong or improving, it is important to reinforce what is working well and not just rest on your laurels. This can make trust a strategic advantage for the organization and fully leverage its benefits. In the scenario that the scores are decreasing or low, you or some team leader needs to dig into the numbers more, summarize the findings, and develop a plan to correct the core issues that drove the low trust scores.

Similar to the organizational support needed to make trust a metric on the company scorecard, a coordinated and targeted improvement plan needs strong endorsement from senior management to be executed with the energy and resources to be successful. While changing trust scores will not happen overnight, a thoughtful plan executed well will clearly make a difference.

Two key dangers to avoid when putting together the analysis and communication plan for the scores include (1) motivating employees indirectly or directly to inflate trust scores and (2) overreacting to changes in scores that are not statistically significant. The goal of a diagnostic survey is to uncover or confirm information that can be used to better manage the team or organization. When those answering the survey receive a benefit such as a 1% increase in bonus when trust scores increase, the value and credibility of the survey tool are greatly weakened. As a result, the manager or leader is not any better in managing the organization than before initiating the survey. In fact, they are in a worse position due to the inability to use the diagnostic tool going forward.

For teams or organizations that are small, survey instruments should be interpreted cautiously due to low sample sizes. For teams of twenty-five people or fewer, each individual represents at least 4% of the total, meaning that just a few responses can significantly affect the results. The same difference of 4% for a much larger organization could point to a major finding. That is why the concept of statistical significance should be applied in reviewing the results. Statistical significance is a measure of how likely your scores are different from a comparative set or a baseline due to random chance alone. There is no point in getting excited or upset if the change in trust scores from last year to this year are not statistically significant as the difference is within the normal variation of doing such surveys.

Given the cost in administrating surveys and concerns with interpreting scores, many organizations will not be able to agree on making trust an important company measure even when they believe in its value. When struggling with the decision internally, another way to motivate the adoption of trust score measurement is to involve customers. Imagine the impact of someone's top customer telling the organization that they cannot trust them or their brand is untrustworthy. That will quickly get people's attention and move trust high up on the radar. This approach has been applied by many companies, transforming how they are viewed externally and often reshaping how they act internally with each other.[81]

Unfortunately, measuring trust is not as straightforward as finding out whether a company that you are negotiating with will accept your offer for a $200 million milestone payment, as I found out. Yet, without trust, you may never even ask.

Winning Moves

Develop and execute a plan to monitor the trust level in your organization over time, gaining agreement from all meaningful levels of the organization.

- ▶ Solve for areas of low trust and communicate those efforts back to the organization.
- ▶ Establish predictable and consistent communication schedules with employees.
- ▶ Be thoughtful about monitoring remote workers to get no more than the information needed.

- ► Consider incorporating trust as a companywide measure to increase its priority.
- ► Understand whether customers view your organization or key product as being trustworthy.

9

A CRISIS OF CREDIBILITY

IMAGINE YOU WORK FOR A COMPANY that takes one of its most popular and revenue-producing drugs off the market because of concerns over side effects. I didn't have to imagine.

As head of investor relations, I was responsible for reporting the company's quarterly earnings and answering questions, along with executive management when they attended, to the public, including the financial analysts who monitored the company. My department and I took this responsibility seriously and went to great lengths to verify any information that was to be presented. Analysts used such interactions, especially those that were open to the public, to ask challenging questions that not only addressed important issues but also demonstrated their expertise in following the company.

After introductions, we opened every interaction with a disclosure called Forward Looking Statements that essentially communicated that anything that was discussed about the future was far from certain and simply our best understanding of the situation. While this practice was a necessary protection against liability, it also acknowledged that, despite our best efforts, nothing in the future was guaranteed.

While I was in the role, the company decided to withdraw a popular product, with sales of over $1 billion, due to a limited but potential risk of causing cardiovascular events such as heart attacks. The impact on the stock price was immediate and substantial, with billions of dollars in market capitalization lost after the announcement. A competitor with a similar product decided to not withdraw their product, which created even more pressure on my team to explain our decision. Further complicating matters, the potential for class action lawsuits, whether justified or not, increased the pressure to be precise in our communications.

The initial few weeks after the announcement were long days for our team. Ranging from large institutional firms to individuals holding only a few shares, it seemed everyone wanted to vent regarding the money they had lost and how we could have managed the situation better. Importantly, we were unified on clear and concise talking points from which we could respond, even though most people who called us preferred that we just listen. I believe that by listening to their individual stories, we regained some of the trust that had been lost.

I remember talking to a highly respected analyst from a major bank who did not agree with the company's decision to withdraw the product and downgraded the company's stock. Instead of avoiding his questions, in every interaction with him, I stressed the known facts and considerations that a company needs to make in such circumstances. I never took his criticisms personally and matched his persistence with a patient consistency that ultimately led to mutual respect for our different perspectives.

While he never changed his public position on the product withdrawal, during the next opportunity in which he evaluated a major company milestone, the launch of a new product, he was exceptionally favorable in his evaluation. I will never know if our interactions over the more difficult issue influenced him to be more positive in his subsequent review, but I know that it certainly did not hurt.

The Noise and the Narrative

As a leader or someone who is trying to build or maintain trust, you cannot ignore the role and influence of the media due to its ability to shape the perspectives and attitudes of the people with whom you are trying to engage. The media serve important functions to society including providing information, educating individuals, supplying entertainment, and connecting people or organizations, including the government. Not long ago, the media were seen to be the primary source of reliable information, helping to build trust or highlighting untrustworthy behavior by informing the public about current events, policies, and important social issues.

When media outlets provide accurate, fact-based reporting, they enhance trust in both the media itself and in the institutions they cover.[82] Conversely when the media broadcast half-truths or misinformation, the damage to the people or organizations involved can be significant. It can be especially devastating for companies whose reputations are central to their success, particularly consumer-driven businesses with many competitors, such as restaurants.

Investigative journalism, a key component of the news media, historically helps build a strong reputation for the media and through its exposés has played a vital role in maintaining transparency and accountability in society. By uncovering corruption, misconduct, or malpractice, media outlets can either bolster trust in institutions (by ensuring checks and balances) or erode it (when exposing institutional failures). For example, reporting on scandals such as the Watergate investigation or the Catholic Church abuse scandals led to significant declines in trust in those institutions.[83]

In addition to investigative journalism, the media through their timely updates can shape how people view government, corporations, the judiciary, and other societal institutions. Positive or negative coverage can directly impact public perceptions of these entities.[84] For example, critical reporting on government waste or policy delays can diminish public trust in government institutions, while highlighting successes and transparency efforts can boost confidence. As a result of its choices of what information to communicate to its audiences, the media are often blamed for providing subjective coverage and perceived as having political or ideological biases. This can contribute to a polarized media landscape, where audiences selectively trust outlets that align with their own beliefs.

In countries like the US, media have played a major role in widening the trust gap between political groups, with each political party favoring information sources from different cable new channels, for example. In a self-reinforcing relationship, the media will prioritize stories that reflect the biased interest of their viewers to better serve them, much like any business would address the needs of its customers. According to a Pew

Research Center study, Republicans and Democrats trust different news sources, with conservatives gravitating toward right-leaning outlets (like Fox News or OANN) and liberals toward left-leaning outlets (like CNN or MSNOW). This selective trust reinforces echo chambers, where individuals only consume media that align with their views.[85]

Besides differences in political groups, significant gaps in trust have emerged by age over the past several years concerning the media. People younger than fifty are much less trusting of the news media than people aged fifty and older, particularly the oldest Americans (those aged sixty-five and older). An analysis of the last few years of data shows a 17-point gap in trust between the oldest Americans (those aged sixty-five and older) and those under age fifty—43% vs. 26%, respectively.[86] This gap does not bode well for the long-term, sustainable role for media.

The rise of misinformation, disinformation, and "fake news"—especially online and through social media platforms—has severely damaged trust in both media and the institutions being reported on.[87] When false information spreads, it undermines the credibility of legitimate news sources and creates confusion about which sources can be trusted. This may seem counterintuitive: The result of misinformation typically does not lead to the false content being evaluated as credible. Instead, the greater tendency is to disbelieve both fake and true messages. The spillover effects of misinformation in the media have been used to explain disengagement with news media in general and distrust in traditional news institutions.[88]

Social media platforms play a growing role in influencing trust among individuals. In 2025, just over half of US adults (53%) say they at least sometimes get news from social media, up significantly from the past decade, according to the Pew Research Center.[89] Social media platforms provide a way for people to connect and build relationships, often promoting trust within online communities. Users can engage with like-minded individuals, share experiences, and form supportive networks that may enhance interpersonal trust. For example, communities on platforms like TikTok or Reddit often build strong, trust-based relationships among members through shared interests or causes.[90]

Conversely, social media can erode interpersonal trust by enabling anonymity and the potential for misrepresentation. People can hide behind fake profiles or selectively present their lives in ways that distort reality, leading to skepticism about others' authenticity.[91] The superficiality of many interactions on social media also leads to trust relationships that may be more fragile compared to face-to-face relations.

Social media algorithms typically show users the content that aligns with their existing beliefs and preferences, creating echo chambers where people are primarily exposed to viewpoints they already agree with.[92] This can reduce trust in those outside their immediate circle and deepen divisions among social, political, or ideological groups. Research has shown that polarized social media environments can heighten hostility and reduce trust across political, social, or cultural lines.[93] Even families celebrating Thanksgiving together increasingly tell of arguments breaking out when touching on political or controversial subjects.

The algorithms have worked so well that you can clearly identify gender, education, political and other disproportionate clusters of users around each major site. For example, women make up greater portions of regular news consumers on Nextdoor (64%), TikTok (62%), Facebook (60%), Snapchat (60%), and Instagram (59%), while men make up greater shares on Reddit (68%), X (64%), Rumble (60%), Truth Social (58%), and YouTube (57%).[94]

Concerning other disproportionate audiences, 48% of news consumers on WhatsApp are Hispanic, and LinkedIn has the largest portion of news consumers with a college degree (55%). Finally, regarding political affiliation, overwhelming shares of regular news consumers on Truth Social (88%) and Rumble (83%) are Republicans or Republican-leaning independents. With such disproportionate audiences, it is natural for those social media outlets to focus their news filters on information that appeals to those audiences.

A survey of over 10,000 US adults, conducted by the Pew Research Center explored how social media impacts trust among individuals and found that heavy social media use often leads to lower levels of interpersonal trust.[95] Frequent users were more likely to report lower levels of trust in others compared to those who used social media less frequently. The anonymity and selective presentation of information on social media contributed to this decline, as users were often unsure about the authenticity of others online.

Similar to the Pew Research study, the Knight Foundation and Gallup surveyed 1,440 Gallup Panel members to assess how pervasive US adults believe bias in news reporting is, and whether they make distinctions between bias and inaccuracy.[96] The study found that most Americans perceive news on social media as biased or less reliable compared to traditional news outlets, with 60% of respondents saying they had little to no trust in the news they saw on social media, with concerns about misinformation and echo chambers contributing to this distrust.

In comparing media alternatives, the Edelman Trust Barometer showed that social media is the least trusted sector, with trust in social platforms declining globally to 42%, below search engines (62%), traditional media (58%), and owned media (47%).[97] The rise of fake news and concerns over how platforms moderate content (or fail to do so) are cited as significant factors contributing to this lack of trust.

Once a critical source for news and clarifying misinformation, trust in traditional media (such as newspapers, TV news) has been declining in many countries as well. In the US, for instance, only 31% of adults expressed trust in the news media in 2024, according to the Gallup poll, down from 72% in the 1970s.[98] This decline is due to several factors, including perceived political bias, sensationalism, and the rise of alternative information sources.

Increasingly, the public views media outlets as being influenced by political, corporate, or ideological agendas. Only 52% of the respondents from the Edelman Trust Barometer in 2025 said they trusted the media overall, with many citing bias and sensationalism as reasons for their mistrust. When media outlets are perceived as prioritizing profits or pushing particular narratives, public trust in their objectivity erodes.[99] It is no secret that many news outlets are known for being either left leaning, such as CNN and MSNOW, or right leaning, such as Fox, which creates skepticism that they are simply reporting the news and not pushing a certain agenda.

The COVID-19 pandemic serves as a tremendous example of the pivotal role of media in shaping public trust in health institutions and scientific authorities only a few years ago.[100] Studies found that trust in traditional media, including public service broadcasters and established news outlets, was associated with greater willingness to follow COVID-19 regulations and higher perceptions of the seriousness of the pandemic. In contrast, greater reliance on non-traditional or social media was linked to increased belief in conspiracy theories and lower compliance with public health measures. Immediately after the COVID-19 pandemic, according to the Edelman Trust Barometer in 2022, trust in healthcare institutions fell dramatically in many countries where mixed messages and misinformation flourished.[101]

The rise of alternative media platforms, including blogs, podcasts, and independent news channels, has diversified the media landscape and created millions of new options to consume media.[102] These platforms often appeal to niche audiences by offering viewpoints that differ from mainstream outlets. While they can build strong trust among certain groups, they may also contribute to fragmentation and reduced trust in traditional media institutions. Many of these alternative sources have been linked to the spread of misinformation or partisan viewpoints, which can further erode trust in the broader media ecosystem.

Another trend in media is found in citizen journalism—where regular individuals report on events via social media or blogs—which can also influence trust. While first-person accounts empower individuals to share direct accounts and information, it can also blur the line between professional journalism and unverified information. Trust in citizen journalism varies depending on its alignment with traditional journalistic standards, such as fact-checking and editorial oversight.[103]

Even more than citizen journalism, the emergence of "news influencers" over the last ten years has disrupted the traditional way people consume the news. Influencers rely on the trust they have built up with their audiences to extend to the information they are presenting. A Pew

Research Center study in 2024 looked at such influencers who are defined as individuals who regularly post about current events and civic issues on social media and have at least 100,000 followers on any of Facebook, Instagram, TikTok, X, or YouTube.

The study found that about one in five Americans, including 37% of adults under thirty, responded that they regularly get news from influencers on social media. Despite greater than three-fourths of influencers having no affiliation with any news organization or background, 65% of the consumers of their information report that news influencers on social media have helped them better understand current events and civic issues.[104]

With all these outlets for news media catering to specific interests, the ability to critically evaluate media content is essential for building trust in the right sources. Media literacy initiatives, which teach individuals how to discern reliable information from misinformation or biased reporting, are increasingly important in today's media environment.[105] Higher levels of media literacy can help individuals navigate the vast array of information available online and foster informed trust in credible media outlets.

Several studies suggest that improving media literacy can restore trust in media by helping people recognize trustworthy sources and understand how news is produced.[106] In one of the more comprehensive studies, Impress, a British organization focused on promoting confidence in news, surveyed over 3,000 UK residents and carried out in-depth focus group work in March 2022.[107]

When asked what journalists must do to get a story published, no requirement was selected by more than 52% of the respondents. More directly related to trust, only 50% of people believe that publishers must verify the facts or assess the truth of a story to get it published. Additionally, less than half believe that journalists are required to be balanced, unbiased, or use multiple sources, and 17% either don't know or believe that none of these requirements apply.

Given this lack of awareness of the journalism process and the impact on the trust in media as a result, governments and educational institutions have begun prioritizing media literacy as part of broader efforts to combat misinformation and rebuild public trust in journalism.[108]

Another way media organizations are working to rebuild trust is by increasing transparency around their reporting processes. Fact-checking initiatives and transparent sourcing of information help demonstrate a commitment to accuracy and integrity.[109] A few leading US newspapers began implementing and promoting fact-checking mechanisms in 2017 to ensure credibility and regain public trust, with many other legacy news companies following suit in subsequent years.[110]

After growing 140% from 2016 to 2022, the number of global fact-checking sites started to level off in 2023.[111] This tactic has been marginally beneficial in improving trust levels in media, with many citing selective use of the fact-checking as a way to minimize its impact.[112] As a result, while people may become more accurate in their beliefs through fact-checking, they can also grow more skeptical or even cynical about the media's motives and fairness.

With greater skepticism concerning fact-checking, social media platforms have also largely withdrawn fact-checking algorithms and replaced them with community policing. Meta (Facebook), Google (YouTube), and TikTok have made decisions in 2025 that essentially ended their fact-checking of news content.[113] Even the US government, whose Counter Foreign Information Manipulation and Interference Hub at the State Department, formerly known as the Global Engagement Center, had been responsible for policing misinformation, decided to walk away from such efforts and closed in April 2025.[114]

Trust in the media itself is not so important to individuals, organizations, or the government, but when people cannot rely on a common source of accurate information, it makes any task involving broad communication harder, especially if it is a complex or controversial message. As seen in the Trustworthy Decision Matrix, a project that has a high degree of difficulty should only be executed by organizations or individuals who have a consistent track record of meeting expectations, unless the downside of failure is low.

As current media channels make any large communication effort harder, we are likely forgoing numerous meaningful efforts that otherwise would have been executed due to a poorly functioning media system. Leaders will increasingly need to take the inefficiency of the media into account as they guide their organizations, regardless of industry or purpose.

As difficult as any product withdrawal is, my experience as head of investor relations would have become exponentially more challenging in today's information age due to the distrust that exists across the media and the plethora of talking heads and influencers who seek to galvanize their audiences. It places even greater importance in being transparent with a consistent and clear-cut story. While the media environment certainly has changed and made any implementation harder, the basics of communicating a consistent and clear message that can be trusted remains the same.

The Bottom Line

The media have a significant influence on public trust on multiple levels, whether in shaping trust in institutions, interpersonal relationships, or even trust in the media itself. The rise of misinformation, media polarization, and the perception of bias have led to declining trust in many parts of the world. The lowest trust scores come from people who are under age fifty and have more experience with social media and alternative media outlets.

Social media platforms significantly contribute to the erosion in trust in legacy media. Through their use of echo chambers, social media platforms, including citizen journalism and news influencers, they serve information that is filtered consistent with the prejudices of their users, which allows them to reinforce existing beliefs and block news that would otherwise make it easier to critically assess the information landscape. This selectivity results in high trust scores within the user community and low trust scores when going outside the community.

At the same time, media outlets, including social media, have the potential to rebuild trust across society by focusing on transparency, accuracy, and media literacy. Fact-checking and other tactics proved helpful for a short time, before their own claims of bias led to significant mistrust. The media's evolving role in trust-building highlights the importance of responsible journalism and the challenges of the informed consumption of news. Companies need to be increasingly adept to manage communications and reputations in this more fragmented, distrustful environment.

The So What

Why should a business leader care about whether the media can be trustworthy? Much of the focus of the news is not relevant to your organization, and only a small fraction of organizations are ever mentioned. Even public companies have modest reporting requirements that rarely interest the general population. Leaders have too many other issues that need their focus to care about the media, right?

Two critically important groups make it worthwhile for corporate leaders to keep tabs on how trustworthy the media are: its customers and employees. Customers often decide to engage or purchase from an organization based on its reputation. That is the fundamental basis for why an organization engages the media to convey a message, such as brand promotion or developing an organizational image. How trustworthy the source is greatly determines its viability as an effective communication vehicle. For example, if 95% of golfers trust the reporting of *Golf Digest*, the manufacturers of golf balls should consider placing advertisements within that journal. On the other hand, if only 5% of golfers trust *Golf Digest*, it probably does not make sense to place the same communication.

Yet much of the information that customers learn about a product does not come directly from the company, especially regarding consumer products. The explosive growth of consumer blogs, reviews and ratings on Amazon, Yelp, or Trustpilot, for example, and social media content can create overnight boom or busts depending on what is said, who says it, and how widely it is picked up. As you may recall, the leader of the Taco Bell organization had to develop an effective strategy to respond to viral rumors of the franchise using "Grade D" beef for its products.[115] It did not matter that the viral posts had no credibility as the USDA doesn't even use letter grades like "Grade D" for ground or seasoned beef products because customers started to trust the accusation. The viability of the company can be at stake due to the power of the media, whether based on accurate information or not.

That is why certain established sources, such as legacy media or top-tier social influencers, can play a critical role in putting out fires or, unfortunately, fanning the flames of emerging rumors due to the trust of their audiences and their associated reach. You need to ensure that your organization has a way to access such a trusted source to protect against the downside of viral rumors or to capitalize on legitimate upsides. Knowing which sources are trusted makes a big difference in effectively managing the situation. The declining trust in legacy media clearly weakens its viability in some situations, but still should not be dismissed. Monitoring social media for mention of your company or its products is critical to even understand if there is an opportunity that needs to be addressed.

Besides customers, employees are the second major group of stakeholders that require leaders to keep a pulse on the media. Employees want to work for a company with a strong, honest reputation. Negative media stories or misleading social posts can alter those perceptions. When an organization gets negative reviews or is embroiled in controversy, it is harder to keep employees engaged.

This becomes an even more difficult situation when a significant number of the employees are filtering out established media channels and relying on more radical social media platforms for their information. Due to the echo chambers and self-supporting communities that comprise some of these social networks, it is hard for employees who are part of these networks to trust information outside of their networks, especially from an employer. As a result, false rumors on social media can prove problematic to overcome and must be addressed early and directly to the employee base to prevent it from spreading from a small subset of employees to those who are not part of the infectious social network. Rumors or viral posts can even trigger high turnover as in the Wayfair ethics walkout in which a viral post of a furniture order headed to a federal migrant detention center caused about 10% of the headquarters staff to walk out.[116]

Recognizing that employees have embraced the use of social media, some companies actually have built their own internal sites to support information sharing in an effort to create a more vibrant community feel within the organization. This can work well, especially if employees adhere to the rules associated with the company networks, such as maintaining confidential information and restricting the content to work- or employee-related information. Like external social media sites, if the users feel they are being monitored or the information is inappropriately being filtered, their trust in the site will be low and subsequently its utilization will be negligible.

While positive employee perceptions of the company help them to be inclined to trust the organization and motivated to contribute to its goals, a strong reputation is also critical to attract desirable talent in a competitive employee marketplace. If surveys posted on the internet consistently show employee satisfaction is low, top employee talent will think twice about joining that organization given the ease in searching for such information.

Organizations that treat their employees poorly should be exposed in a highly efficient market environment. Trying to use social media or other communication channels to sugarcoat the problem may work short term but will ultimately make the correction harder as it will undermine the credibility of the company's word. To put it differently, when you have a flat tire, it is better to take the time to pull over and replace it versus telling the passengers that the road seems to be more bumpy than usual.

Winning Moves

Be aware of how and where you and your team consume media and the potential bias that exists.

- ► Obtain news from multiple, diverse media sources to gain more perspective on how others may be viewing events.
- ► Do not simply filter out information that is not consistent with your views.
- ► Encourage others to improve their media literacy to better flag false information.
- ► Monitor company and brand reputation on social media to ensure positive perceptions that will reinforce employee retention and complement recruiting efforts.

10

IT ALL STARTS WITH YOU

After I graduated from college, I accepted a job offer to work for a major railroad company within their fast-track leadership program for high-potential employees. My initial role was a challenging one: to introduce sustainable technology that would be supported by management and union leaders and improve productivity and company goodwill. While there were certainly bumps along the way, I proved to be quite effective in saving the company money and reducing employee frustration in a way that was readily acceptable by the union and non-union employees.

Within my first year, I was promoted twice and presented to the CEO some of the projects. Over the next few years, I gained valuable leadership experience in MIS and finance, ultimately being asked to redesign the company's internal costing system, which would determine the profitability of customer routes, guide pricing of new contracts, and calculate bonuses for sales management. Leading such a strategic and core company system design, I was able to network across the various functional leaders and built a tremendous support system for advocacy.

Besides more than doubling my salary and becoming a common presenter to senior management, including the CEO, I built important friendships along the way. The future seemed extremely bright for my career. Yet the company decided to relocate its headquarters from Minneapolis to Dallas. Although it would probably take a few years, I would need to relocate to Texas in order to advance my career to the levels that I was being groomed for. I was now married and with a newborn son, so the decision was going to be important for our family. While Texas is a great place, it was not in the top ten lists for my wife given that her family was still in the upper Midwest and she had lived in northern climates all her life.

About that time, a third-party headhunter reached out to me concerning a job in Pennsylvania working in the pharmaceutical industry. The recruiter was a specialist in finding analytical expertise for retained searches and came across my background within SAS (analytics and artificial intelligence software) congresses and other sources. The position was in marketing, which I was exposed to at the railroad and within my evening MBA program sponsored by the railroad company. I knew very little about pharmaceuticals, but the location of the main office was about an hour away from where I went to high school. While my parents and many high school friends had moved from the area, it was still a quite acceptable setting to live in.

I needed to decide among three main alternatives: (1) do nothing and continue to work in Minneapolis, (2) make the move to Dallas to stay with the comfortable and supportive knowns of the railroad company and likely future success, or (3) move to Pennsylvania for a new job function and a new company, which had a good reputation but no one I personally knew. Each option had key supportive arguments, but I was focused on the options to move to Dallas or Pennsylvania because staying in Minneapolis was not sustainable long-term.

One of the biggest factors in making the decision between these two options was concerning my belief whether I could be successful in marketing and in the pharmaceutical industry. I really did not know, and it was a big gamble to give up on a rising career with a high probability of success for the unknowns associated with the other choice. I was fortunate that my wife was supportive of either path that I selected, but I clearly knew her preference for cold winters over hot summers.

While there were many factors, the career decision ultimately came down to whether I had trust in myself to learn a new profession and industry or were the knowns of my current situation too compelling to give up. Ultimately, I took the gamble because I believed I could succeed. Over twenty-five years later with that company and over thirty years in the life sciences industry, I feel confident that I made the right decision.

The Trust Within

Self-trust—the confidence in your own judgment, abilities, and instincts—is shaped by a complex interplay of psychological, social, and experiential factors.[117] It's about believing that you can handle whatever comes your way. Self-trust means you listen to your inner voice, make choices that align with your values, and stand by those choices—even if others disagree or the outcome is uncertain. It's the foundation that allows you to act authentically and take risks, knowing you can cope with the results. High self-trust allows better decision-making, greater resilience when faced with any setbacks, increased motivation and initiative, and healthier relationships.[118]

It is easy to confuse self-trust with either self-esteem or self-confidence. Self-esteem is your overall sense of self-worth. It's how much you value yourself as a person, regardless of your achievements or what others think of you. High self-esteem means you feel deserving of happiness, respect, and love. It's about accepting yourself, flaws and all, and believing that you are fundamentally valuable. By contrast, low self-esteem makes it difficult for you to think of yourself as something other than a victim of your flaws and can lead to depression and other mood disorders.[119]

Self-confidence is the belief in your ability to succeed in specific situations or tasks. It is not always there but context dependent; for example, you might feel confident giving a presentation at work but not as confident in interacting with friends. Self-confidence tends to grow as you gain experience and succeed in areas of your life. Low self-confidence makes it harder for you to do something that you have not done before as you anticipate failure or negative feedback.[120]

Self-trust starts early in life as you experience success and failure in trying new things. It is not necessarily whether you succeed or not that builds self-trust, but how you and others respond to the attempt. Supportive, consistent, and nurturing environments foster self-trust, while inconsistent, critical, or neglectful caregiving can plant seeds of self-doubt.[121]

As a person matures, experiences, especially successes, achievements, and positive feedback continue to build self-trust. Even if you did not have a strong sense of self-trust as a youth, you can still develop it as an adult. While self-trust does not require that you succeed all the time, the less you accomplish puts more pressure on the need to have a supportive environment that helps you through any failures.

Conversely, failures, setbacks, and criticism can erode self-trust, especially if these experiences are internalized as reflections of personal worth or ability. Based on our predispositions, we may have a distorted perspective that the failure was due to our actions or others. Peer feedback is important to refine our understanding of what happened and whether our role meaningfully affected the outcome.[122] Without peer feedback, patterns like confirmation bias, seeking evidence for self-doubt, self-serving interpretations, or attributing failures to external factors can undermine or exaggerate self-trust.

Even though it is often not acknowledged, people are constantly talking to themselves. Ensuring that the self-talk is positive can be a key driver to healthy self-trust. The evidence supporting positive self-talk has been extensively developed, which explains why self-talk is widely advocated for performance enhancement in sports, academic engagement, and regulating anxiety or depression in a clinic.[123] While positive internal dialogue reinforces self-trust, focusing on flaws or the potential for failure undermines it. While it is easier to say than do, you should try to have a healthy balance of self-criticism and encouragement when you talk with yourself.

Although people's natural tendencies may be looking at a glass half empty, in terms of self-trust, it helps to have a positive attitude and see the glass as half full. Researchers have explored the effects of positive thinking and optimism on health, much of which is reinforced through self-talk.[124] Health benefits associated with positive thinking range from better psychological and physical well-being to better cardiovascular health and reduced risk of death from cardiovascular disease and stroke. It is unclear why people who engage in positive thinking experience improved health benefits, although researchers have postulated that having a positive outlook enables you to better cope with stressful situations, which reduces the harmful health effects of stress on your body.

One way to improve the awareness and implementation of supportive self-trust is to practice mindfulness and journaling to understand your thoughts and feelings. Mindfulness can potentially alter how you experience emotions because it teaches you to observe and accept in a non-judgmental manner, rather than immediately react to your thoughts and feelings.[125] As a result, mindfulness is helpful when you experience emotions like disappointment and anger by recognizing the emotion and removing some of its negative energy.

Similar to mindfulness, studies by James Pennebaker and Joshua Smyth, among others, have shown that writing about emotional experiences helps you process and organize your thoughts and feelings, leading to greater mental clarity and resilience.[126] This research consistently found that expressive writing and journaling can reduce stress, improve mood, and enhance self-understanding, all of which contribute to stronger self-trust. If you have not tried journaling or mindfulness, you should consider exploring such techniques given all the research that supports it.

Despite methods to reinforce self-trust, the pursuit of perfection undermines many of them and can make you overly critical of yourself, which leads to chronic self-doubt and reluctance to trust your own decisions. In research on perfectionism and mental health, self-oriented perfectionism was associated with a number of psychological disorders and symptoms (such health conditions as anorexia, bulimia, obsessive beliefs, and worry).[127] A key takeaway is that you must have reasonable expectations and accept mistakes to have a healthy mind.

Additionally, fear of making mistakes or failing can inhibit self-trust and set you up to create a cycle where lack of trust in yourself leads to more mistakes. Atelophobia is an obsessive fear of imperfection in which you are so terrified of making mistakes that you tend to avoid any situation where you feel you will not succeed.[128] This condition can lead to anxiety, depression, and low self-esteem. Even in less moderate cases, fear of making mistakes can prevent growth because we cannot learn without making mistakes.[129] With self-compassion, cognitive strategies, and support, it is possible to reduce this fear and develop self-trust in situations that entail some risk. For example, my colleague who was fearful of presenting to the management group overcame her fear (and on a laptop in the dark no less). Do you have any fears that are preventing you from growth?

Societal norms, cultural expectations, and family beliefs can condition you to mistrust your instincts, especially if your desires conflict with external expectations.[130] For example, if women in certain societies are not expected to be experts in math or engineering, they may be reluctant to trust themselves in managing a budget or solving analytical problems. Societies may also underappreciate the role of the individual and overemphasize the group, such that you depend on others for decision-making or validation. Such cultural norms may serve to weaken your exposure to experiences that would otherwise develop self-trust. When a company's social norms serve to simply protect itself from criticism or change, disaster will soon follow. For example, the groupthink at Kodak drove a collective resistance to emerging technology, despite tremendous intelligence that digital photos would become the industry standard in the near future, resulting in bankruptcy for this industry leader in 2012.[131]

Can the Trustworthy Decision Matrix work for self-trust? Of course, it can, if you can be objective in assessing your own trustworthiness. For example, for the decision of whether I should accept the job in Pennsylvania, the matrix would suggest that if I was trustworthy, that the decision would depend on the difficulty of the transition and the ability to have support in making the transition. Fortunately, I had tremendous support from my wife and family, and the new company provided me with the resources and reasonable expectations to succeed, which validates the decision that I made

The Bottom Line

Self-trust is about relying on your own judgment and staying true to yourself. Self-trust is highly correlated and reinforced by self-esteem and self-confidence. While these attributes are related and can influence each other, each plays a unique role in your personal development and well-being.

Positive experiences, supportive self-talk, realistic expectations, and validating peer feedback can be helpful in developing sustainable self-trust. Obstacles to achieving self-trust include self-criticism, past failure or trauma, perfectionism, and overreliance on others' opinions or societal norms that devalue the individual. Self-trust is built over time, starting as early as childhood, and often requires effort and focus to achieve. Once gained, high self-trust allows better decision-making, greater resilience when faced with any setbacks, increased motivation and initiative, and the promotion of healthier relationships.

The So What

Self-trust is pivotal for leaders to be able to effectively manage others and maintain effectiveness through the inevitable ups and downs that occur within a team and organization. You can be the most talented individual in your field yet not be able to motivate others or survive challenges to their opinions without self-trust. If managers don't trust themselves, it's hard for others to trust them, and even harder for them to lead effectively. That is why we don't often find self-trust as being a major weakness for established leaders.

Yet what about leaders who have too much self-trust? It turns out that having too much self-trust can be just as damaging for business leaders as having too little. When confidence crosses into overconfidence, a leader's decision-making and ability to adapt can be compromised. This will ultimately restrict a leader to be trusted only for easy or low-risk projects based on the Trustworthy Decision Matrix due to a lack of a reliable feedback mechanism that can correct oversights.

To be an effective decision-maker, you have to first be able to accurately assess a given situation to determine the best course of action. It is tough enough for a leader to learn of problems or challenges that need to be resolved because of the perception that the bad news may reflect on the individual who raises it. It certainly does not help when excessive self-trust causes managers to rely too heavily on their instincts and ignore data. "Been there, done that" is fine for simple, recurring issues, yet in today's fast-changing, technology-driven environment, few people can simply rely on their experience to be an effective leader without digging into the situation.

Even after assessing the relevant background, a leader with too much self-trust may tune out advice or suggested solutions from others. The belief that they "know best" stifles alternative perspectives and new insights necessary to arrive at the best decision. This can lead to biased or uninformed decisions, while also limiting innovation and team engagement. Too much faith in your own judgment can result in underestimating risks or overestimating capabilities. Managers may skip the necessary due diligence or fail to prepare contingency plans when they feel that their gut knows better.

Employees do not want to work for someone who is resistant to feedback or their ideas. This may lead to a feeling of being undervalued or ignored, undermining collaboration and psychological safety. The leader may lose the trust of their team and not even realize it. Execution of projects may miss key milestones, and negative morale may set in.

These downsides arise even when the overly confident leader's decision turns out to be correct. When the decision is poor, the consequences multiply and lead to an even longer list of negatives. Over-trusting managers may rationalize failures rather than reflect on them, repeating the same errors instead of improving. They may insulate themselves from blame and in turn criticize the execution of others. Without the ability to learn from mistakes, the leader is more likely to repeat those failures or at least not reduce the risk or reoccurrence.

Excessive self-confidence can create a sense of moral invincibility—believing "my intentions are good, so my actions are justified." This can lead to ethical lapses or reputational damage. The leader may have a very different risk-and-reward tradeoff equation than the rest of the company, which puts the company at some risk. Those who take direction from the leader will observe the disconnect first, yet without a manager being receptive to feedback, it may not change the course of action.

How can an organization guard against leaders having too much self-trust? The best ways are to ensure effective oversight and feedback channels. The leader may be blind to their own behavior, yet with appropriate oversight and review from higher management or peers may be able to adjust their decision-making to be more evidence-based and collaborative. Quite frankly, individuals, including you, need to be able to step up and proclaim the emperor has no clothes, without fear of retribution. Mentors can have an enormously valuable role here to help leaders achieve the right balance of self-trust. Otherwise, too much self-trust turns confidence into arrogance, and reduces openness, empathy, and accountability—the very qualities that sustain strong leadership and organizational trust.

Fortunately, when I made the career decision to transition to the pharmaceutical industry, I had a wife who was more than willing to tell me if I was crazy in evaluating the options. Still, self-trust was essential to give me the courage to make the move and also critical to succeed once the decision was made.

Winning Moves

Evaluate if your self-trust is supportive or holding you back.

- ▶ Work to have a supportive set of friends or peers who can help provide feedback to confirm or correct self-perceptions.
- ▶ Ensure that you practice and implement positive self-talk.
- ▶ Practice mindfulness and journaling to manage challenges with self-trust.
- ▶ Be aware of having too much self-trust to base decisions solely on gut and rejecting feedback from others.
- ▶ Create a strong and enduring mentor system to fine-tune behaviors and assist in coaching top leaders.

11

STAYING AHEAD OF THE CURVE

I n April 2020, I stopped traveling for business and began to adapt to the new reality of working virtually from home as a result of the COVID-19 pandemic. It was a confusing time for many of us, and unfortunately the pandemic led to many deaths around the world. I tried to learn from the best information available to better advise my family, friends, and others, yet the news concerning the pandemic was incomplete and constantly evolving, even contradictory at times. The sources of the information—both through official and unofficial channels—were not always helpful and often focused their time on criticizing opposing positions versus defining their own positions.

Once the COVID-19 vaccines were granted emergency use authorization and later approved in the US, the amount of information supporting and opposing the vaccines and treatment of COVID-19 was rampant. Given my familiarity with clinical trials and expertise in understanding scientific literature, I tried to keep up with the latest news flow and translate the information into straightforward guidance about the likely risks and benefits to those who were asking for such an opinion. For most people during this period, it was hard to know what we should do, even with expertise and effort, as the data were difficult to assess and far from comprehensive.

One gentleman, who had emigrated from Lithuania and went to the same synagogue as I, asked me. "What do you think about the COVID-19 vaccines? Are they truly safe or not?"

I paused and answered him, "I will send you a note with my thoughts," as it is my experience that when people have trouble with the native language, direct discussion on technical issues is harder to digest than something they can read and translate via computer technology. I took a day or so to provide a clinically based summary of the available information and experience with the COVID-19 vaccines.

I quickly received a reply that had links to various videos. The response basically asked me if I had seen the attached videos before and how those "experts" could be so wrong. I took the time to watch many of the videos, although after the first minute or so had a good sense for their vantage point and information used to support any of their arguments. There were good reasons to question the vaccines, yet these videos were not credible. It was not surprising that this misinformation was out there, but I was stunned to realize that it was being taken so seriously by my trusted peer.

While recognizing that this may not be a productive discussion, I followed up his response by sending an email over the next few days, noting the limitations of some of the arguments, video by video, and data from the clinical trials that yielded the best information to date. I wrote in a way that made the data understandable, even for those with little knowledge of clinical trials, and thought it would help him better see the benefits of the vaccine compared to the risk of COVID-19 for people of his age, during this early stage of the pandemic. I was careful not to be condescending or to pretend to have the judgment of a physician and acknowledged that we were all working with incomplete information. While my summary was far from perfect, I thought it could prove helpful.

It took little time to receive his emailed response in which I am not even sure that he read the points I had spent a fair amount of time to research, crystallize, and break down in a digestible way. Essentially, he just sent me more videos that were of the same type. I should have been able to predict the response, yet perhaps ego got the best of me.

I had confused his intent to learn from another's viewpoint versus convincing me of his viewpoint. I completely understand that people had good reasons to take the COVID-19 vaccine or not take it; the point is that he really had no interest in having an open dialogue. I felt a little guilty of this myself, although I initially tried to learn from his perspective and not simply shut down opposing arguments.

I increasingly observe this type of exchange in my interactions. Trust is not promoted but actually reduced when there is no real openness to the other's ideas. I simply ended the email conversation politely, acknowledging that we were unlikely to agree on the topic and, over time, better clarity would likely become available. It was disappointing to me as I felt that I could have added more value and helped him. Perhaps he thought the same as well. While there was some trust between us, it was no match for videos that aligned with his personal bias and fears.

Evolving Trust Lines

Anybody trying to build a relationship with another person or an organization should have some awareness of trends. It does not mean that you need to wear the latest style of shirt or watch the hottest reality show, but you should not come across as a woolly mammoth that never saw the Ice Age coming. For instance, talking about problems you are having with your phone's landline service may decrease the interest younger people have in seeking your advice. A little awareness goes a long way in shaping the best way to interact with others.

How does this relate to trust? When trying to build trust with others, you need to understand the skepticism or optimism of those whom you are dealing with. Trends help us predict the mood in the room if we have little other background information. By being able to anticipate people's receptiveness to trusting you, you can adjust your talking points or actions to have a greater impact. Please keep in mind that you should never change who you are, as authenticity is critical for being trustworthy, but there is nothing wrong in framing your thoughts to better suit the people you are working with.

While it is easy to conclude that trust levels in general have decreased over time, there is much more to the analysis when looking at relevant details. Trends in trust scores can vary significantly depending on the context—whether you are referring to interpersonal trust, institutional trust, or trust in specific sectors (such as government, media, or corporations). Research from large-scale surveys, such as the Edelman Trust Barometer, Pew Research Center, and World Values Survey, consistently reveals declining trust levels in recent years along with its contributing factors, such that it creates doubt whether the scores will increase in the near future.[132]

Given the recency and magnitude of the COVID-19 pandemic, we cannot escape its impact on trust because the pandemic significantly affected global trust levels across many domains including government institutions, health authorities, political leaders, and even interpersonal trust. Early in the crisis, trust in government and healthcare institutions generally spiked, as people relied on these institutions for guidance. However, as the pandemic continued, and as inconsistencies in responses, misinformation, and vaccine hesitancy emerged, trust began to erode. Many key aspects of the COVID-19 pandemic remain controversial today and likely will remain so in the foreseeable future, but its negative impact on trust is far less debatable.

Multiple studies found a marked decline in trust in government institutions during the pandemic. In the US, trust in the Centers for Disease Control and Prevention (CDC) dropped by about 10% between May and October 2020, with especially significant declines among non-Hispanic White and Hispanic respondents.[133] Trust in the federal government fell more sharply than in state or local governments, with steeper declines among women, Black Americans, those with less education, and Republicans.[134]

Concerning the people running the US government, young people, in particular, experienced a notable erosion of trust in political leaders as a result of the pandemic. This decline in political trust was observed in various countries as well and was often linked to perceptions of poor crisis management.[135] Even the medical community—whose trust scores had been in the highest quartiles for many decades in the US—saw significant erosion in trust in physicians and hospitals with scores declining substantially, dropping from 72% in April 2020 to just 40% by January 2024.[136] This was not isolated to the US as trust toward public health institutions and government handling of the pandemic reported a sharp drop in several countries, notably in Brazil and parts of Europe.

If government officials had used the Trustworthy Decision Matrix or similar tool during the pandemic, they would have understood that they should have only focused new communication efforts on initiatives of low risk because the environment was placing great mistrust in those delivering it. That's why presenting a clear, understandable message through all the noise was going to be difficult. Alternatively, they could have tried to use trusted spokespeople to communicate their message, instead of government officials, which would have made even difficult initiatives possible with additional resources.

While trust eroded in institutions during the pandemic, interpersonal trust actually increased in some countries, including the US. Especially among groups disillusioned with government management of the pandemic, people sought support from their communities and friends instead of institutions, which led to an increase in their trust levels. Within social platforms and emerging media, the shared frustration and beliefs in its causes created strong social bonds and higher interpersonal trust. This was not true universally, as in some countries, notably China, where social trust declined.[137]

Above and beyond the COVID-19 pandemic, an important driver of the decrease in trust has been the evolving role of traditional and emerging media, as initially discussed earlier in this book. While media, largely through investigative reporting, have helped expose reasons for mistrust across society, trust in media and journalism has also been declining, especially in Western countries. The rise of misinformation, political bias, and fake news has led to skepticism about the reliability of news sources. As reported by the Reuters Institute for the Study of Journalism, trust in news had fallen to its lowest levels in countries like the US and the UK in 2022.[138] However, in countries that have maintained high viewership and support for its public broadcasting entities and better control of a unified message, trust in media remains high (in Finland and Norway, for example).

Ironically, fake news or misinformation can be viewed as confirmatory facts by the people who are inclined to share those beliefs—as my friend did who believed those videos about the vaccines. With the proliferation of media options, including citizen journalism and news influencers, or applications that can micro-target small subsets of the population based on ideologies or biases, the ability to filter messages to correspond to these groups has greatly accelerated within the last decade. These echo chambers can build tremendous trust in those sources and within the user groups as the messages amplify self-held beliefs. Are you filtering your news to only view stories that you agree with? If so, you may be sitting in an echo chamber closed to important perspectives.

When someone sees misinformation from different sources, they tend to trust it even more. Trust built on misinformation can be sustainable if the barrier to listening to a different viewpoint is reinforced. This dynamic creates a potentially toxic environment that may take significant change to reverse and could, as with previous, less technologically assisted versions, lead to tremendous hate and tragedy as in the mass murder of millions of Tutsis in 1994, who were falsely accused of being foreigners to Rwanda and spies.[139]

Accelerated by the fragmentation of journalism and its inability to unify around a common truth, trust in institutions, and, specifically, trust in the government has declined in recent years across most countries, beyond what can be attributed to the COVID-19 pandemic. This decline is particularly evident in democratic nations where political polarization, corruption, and perceived inefficiency have contributed to diminishing confidence and would likely have declined even with a well-functioning media.

The COVID-19 pandemic helped to expose some of the weaknesses of the government, which fed the proliferation of anti-government conspiracy theories and creation of many new media outlets. In many countries, political polarization has had a direct impact on trust scores. As a result, trust in government has declined in more than half of the countries surveyed in the Edelman Trust Barometer.[140]

Multiple studies and behavioral experiments confirm that individuals tend to show higher levels of interpersonal trust toward people with the same political affiliation than toward those from opposing parties.[141] Known as partisan trust discrimination, this phenomenon is rooted in social identity and cognitive heuristics: People perceive those with similar attitudes and values as more trustworthy. This polarization also extends to interpersonal trust, where people are more likely to trust those who share their political views.

The trust gap between those on the political left and right is widening, particularly in how each side views government performance and the media. For example, as of May 2024, 35% of Democrats and Democratic-leaning independents said they trust the federal government to do what is right "just about always" or "most of the time," compared to only 11% of Republicans and Republican-leaners in the US.[142] This gap shows no sign of decreasing as media catering to those groups have only amplified their differences.

While trust in governments and media has waned, trust in businesses has generally remained more stable or even increased.[143] Economic stability contributes to increasing trust levels while recessions or other downturns lead to mistrust. For example, after the 2008 financial crisis, trust in financial institutions, banks, and even governments plummeted in many countries.[144] Recovery has been slow, and while trust has largely returned to financial institutions, the growing wealth gap and concerns about economic inequality continue to influence trust scores globally (that is, people of wealth are more likely to trust banks).

People often see corporations, especially large tech firms, as more competent and innovative compared to governmental bodies, which leads to higher trust scores in general. Trust in tech companies, such as PayPal, Apple, Google, and Microsoft, has remained relatively high, but concerns about data privacy, monopolistic behavior, and disinformation on social media platforms like TikTok have led to declining trust in the broader tech sector.[145] These concerns are likely to persist and even increase over time given our dependency on digital technology.

The issue of trust is at the center of the trend for remote working. Remote working has experienced rapid and significant growth since the pandemic. Before 2020, only about 4% of US jobs were remote, but in March 2025, around 23% of the workforce or about one in four Americans work remotely.[146] The trend is especially acute for skilled workers as 43% of American employees with an advanced degree did telework in March 2025 versus only 9% of employees who are high school graduates with no college degree. The trend is here to stay as 36% of US employees would prefer to work fully remote given the choice, more than on-site or hybrid options.

Certain industries, such as professional services, information, and finance, were disproportionately affected by the remote work trend with work rates rising by over 30% between 2019 and 2021, with more than a third of their workforce remaining remote into 2022. Finance and insurance continue to have the largest share of remote workers with 30% of full-time employees in finance and insurance working fully remotely, more than in any other industry, as of March 2025.[147] While the growth was initially due to the pandemic, it remains strong due to strong employee preference for flexibility and the adoption of remote-friendly policies by employers.

Studies support that remote work improves trust with the organization. Research was performed using longitudinal data of 1,000 workers in the UK to show that increasing remote work time was positively related to trust in the organization but not trust in coworkers and managers, who had to manage the situation.[148] The researchers postulated that the act of allowing remote work was a sign of trust by the organization, rather than coworkers or the supervisor, with whom separate agreements needed to be made to ensure the work was performed.

Trust is more crucial and more challenging in remote work environments because without in-person interactions, employees cannot easily build relationships with their manager or peers. The risk of miscommunication, partly due to overreliance on email and text messages, is heightened without the social cues available through in-person interactions. The more time employees spend in remote work arrangements—texting and instant messaging—the more they might feel detached and less committed to their employers. Informal employee information networks and spontaneous communications between manager and employee and with peers is likely reduced.

Like corporations, interpersonal trust has been quite resilient and even grown in many countries over the past decade. In fact, trust in a person that you know has remained relatively stable since 2000 globally, with only a slight decrease from 27% in 2005 to 24% in 2022.[149] For most high-income countries, levels of interpersonal trust have maintained or grown over this period. For example, trust in others is at a record high in the UK, and in the US interpersonal trust has remained stable or slightly increased in recent years.

While it is risky to generalize, the data support that millennials and Gen Zers tend to have lower trust in traditional institutions, including governments and the media, compared to older generations.[150] Exploring this generational data for more clues, according to the Edelman Trust Barometer, less than one-quarter of twenty-year-olds agreed with the statement "most people can be trusted," compared to more than one-third of eighty-year-olds. They are more likely to place trust in businesses, social movements, and nongovernmental organizations (NGOs). Research supports the idea that younger generations are also more skeptical of political leaders and corporate promises, pushing for more transparency and action on issues like climate change, racial inequality, and sustainability.

Conversely, older generations, such as baby boomers and Gen X, tend to have higher levels of trust in institutions like the government, military, and media, though this trust is eroding over time.[151] Older adults also have higher interpersonal trust, reflecting social conditions of earlier decades where communities were often more cohesive. Theories and related research indicate that, as people age, they generally prioritize positive social experiences and relationships, which can foster greater trust. Also reinforcing trust, older adults report higher satisfaction with social ties, more positive interactions, and a greater tendency to focus on the good in others.

Like my friend in my COVID story, he and I were in a similar age range, yet the strength and belief in our different information sources was too strong to forge a bond of trust. Instead of discussing the issue further, we returned to our previous relationship without much interruption. Today, we are much greater friends than we ever were and still have not revisited the topic of COVID-19 vaccines.

The Bottom Line

The performance of trust scores over time is likely our best way to measure trends in trust. These scores are shaped by a wide range of factors, including political polarization, economic crises, institutional performance, and societal change, with the COVID-19 pandemic being one of the events that had the greatest impact in recent years. Information and misinformation, especially during and after the COVID-19 pandemic, have contributed to reduced trust scores. While trust in governments, media, and institutions has generally declined, businesses have fared better, although concerns about privacy and corporate responsibility continue to grow, especially for technological companies.

Interpersonal trust remains high in many contexts and has proven to be quite resilient because people seek connections within their communities and friends during times of change. The greatest source for misinformation, the internet and social media, and the generations that have grown up with it, are also associated with lower trust scores. As social media and their users continue to mature, this trend may moderate as trust tends to increase with age.

The So What

The pace of innovation and change has never been greater, largely driven by technological advances, global interdependence, and social networks. As a result, markets experience significantly more volatility, product life cycles are compressed, and long-term plans inherently entail considerable risk. Although accelerating change brings numerous challenges, it also accelerates adoption of new ideas and products, increases access to cost-effective solutions for reducing inefficiencies, and positions outsourcing as a vital tool for businesses of all sizes.

The more complex your working environment, the more important trust in others becomes to allow people to overcome the emerging chaos. Few companies today operate without outsourcing a core function or collaborating with another organization in a revenue-generating partnership. Do you know where your IT support center is located or who manages your payroll? These areas are often outsourced yet are touchpoints for many employees, when in need.

Even in fully vertically integrated organizations, business managers must rely on their teams, collaborate across functions, and align with leadership to deliver results and manage resources effectively in pursuit of their strategic objectives. Trust is the grease that makes the company's engine operate so that an organization can thrive despite the changes all around them. How many cross-functional teams are created just to ensure alignment and coordination?

Yet trust also is not static as people evolve their views of others over time. In general, trust scores have dropped, especially for people and in organizations that we do not directly know. Millennials and the Gen Zers, which comprise over half of the current workforce, are also less likely to give others the benefit of the doubt until shown otherwise.[152] The increase in remote working models and reduced in-person meetings further constrains the ability to achieve the familiarity that advances trust.

In the midst of all this environmental change and dropping trust levels, how is an organizational leader supposed to leverage trust as the most critical enabler for the company? The answer is not particularly different than it was a few decades ago, although the execution needs to be updated. Essentially, you first need to be trustworthy yourself. By exhibiting the core attributes of trustworthiness, you can build trust within your organization and team and model the way for others. You need to make trust building a priority and measure its score over time to fine-tune efforts.

With higher organizational turnover and more outsourcing, leaders need to dedicate a small but meaningful portion of meetings to introductions for people who have not met before and continue to do so until they sense a familiarity has set in. Organizations need to find ways to get groups of employees or members together physically, whether offering a weekly lunch in the office or quarterly social events during an afternoon or evening. Celebrating successes and milestones becomes even more important in this environment.

Formal communication from leaders needs to be transparent and genuine, leaving little room for misinterpretation. Managers—particularly in person—can adopt a more casual tone aligned with their style and message, but it should still reinforce consistency with past commitments and deliverables to maintain confidence and trust in leadership. You should be proactive in your communications and tend toward overcommunicating as silence can allow doubt to fester and subsets of workers to fill the gaps with their own opinions, which may run counter to the desired message.

Leaders can build and maintain trust that reverses current macro trends by ensuring focus on trust as a goal and executing best practices that have already been established. Without clear focus and disciplined execution, the same forces driving declining trust at global and national levels will inevitably take hold within local organizations and teams. You must proactively address these challenges—because once trust within the organization or company erodes past a tipping point, rebuilding it becomes significantly more difficult.

Winning Moves

Act trustworthy. It is the best, most sustainable strategy to win trust in any environment.

- ▶ Recognize that trends are naturally pulling people to be less trusting, although do not assume so for any individual because there are many competing factors and influences.
- ▶ Communicate proactively and clearly to reduce the likelihood of misinformation.
- ▶ Monitor key sources of social media for misinformation about your organization or company to get ahead of the rapid spread of such information.

- ► Develop strategies to increase familiarity across your organization and teams.
- ► Educate employees and members about the best ways to engage others in virtual meetings or remote settings.

12

SAY IT ISN'T SO, R2-D2

I N October 2024, one of my daughters decided to experience life beyond the East Coast and accepted a role as a travel nurse in the emergency department for a hospital in Portland, Oregon. Having traveled to almost all fifty states and lived in a few, I understood and appreciated the courage and intrigue in living on the other side of the country. I was excited to support her in any way she wanted.

As she needed her car while in Portland and her current apartment in Philadelphia was over 1,000 miles away, I volunteered to go on a cross-country trip with her in which we would drive the car to its new location, while also enjoying some major sites along the way and catching up on things. To maximize the journey, I searched several internet sites for suggested tourist stops to visit and the best routes to avoid traffic delays. While the objective to be maximized was rather straightforward, the number of factors and variables led me to believe that it was an excellent problem for AI to solve. As I was discussing the quest with friends, several mentioned they had used AI for planning their own vacations with surprising success.

With the opportunities in AI being so broad and deep, several AI engines were already available and many more have sprung up since then. I decided to work with ChatGPT, having had some positive experience with it already, and the price, being free, was hard to beat. I asked ChatGPT to maximize our journey from Philadelphia to Portland, trying to stop for meals and staying overnight in established cities.

Like most problems, the more informed the statement to be solved is framed, the richer the quality of the response. As a result, my query now included the number of hours of driving per day, anticipated speed at or under the speed limit, preferred restaurant options, and other details that would make the optimized route much more useful. Getting new results in less than thirty seconds for each iteration was amazing, yet I quickly became numb to the speed and was annoyed if I needed to wait for the recommended solution.

After finalizing the query and coming forward with a few optional routes and plans, I showed them to my daughter, who thought I must have too much time on my hands, and we agreed upon an optimized route through Pittsburgh, visiting Cleveland and Chicago, entering Badlands National Park in South Dakota, exploring Yellowstone National Park, and ultimately to Portland in four full days. Each rest stop, restaurant, and hotel were highlighted in this plan that was put together in less than one hour using AI.

We began our trip on Monday and were making good time, passing through the many construction projects that we would see during the time of year and were ready to stop for lunch. We had passed our planned lunch stop in Pittsburgh an hour earlier, so we simply used Google Maps to search for a good option on the route and ate there. When we arrived at the Rock & Roll Hall of Fame for a break and visit, we already were several hours ahead of the plan.

As we were going through some of the exhibits, I was questioning the utility of the plan we had developed. Although it was still early on the trip, we had been tracking at our assumed miles per hour and were approximately 25% ahead of projections. While being ahead of plan is usually great news, in this case it would require us to adjust all our stops and potentially some overnight reservations.

We took some time to discuss our situation, using Google Maps to provide us real-time updates, and ultimately decided to abandon key parts of our AI-generated map as we had lost trust in its accuracy. We also revisited some previous choices on route preferences and further optimized our choices using more traditional internet searches and logic. With the changes made, we completed the trip in the allotted four days as budgeted and ultimately were not significantly impacted by the need to rewrite our route. The trip turned out to be a great experience for both of us and a necessary way to get her car to Portland.

Reflecting on the choice to use AI for the planning of the trip, I feel it made a lot of sense given the ability of AI to quickly analyze large amounts of data using quantifiable decision criteria and factors. On top of the logic for its use, I had received recommendations that further led me to trust AI for this application. While it remains unknown if the inaccurate plan was due to my user error in prompting or a yet-to-be optimized application of AI, I was so willing to trust its results down to the mile and minute that I did not sufficiently troubleshoot it as I would normally a more conventional approach.

Going forward, while I believe that AI will prove a useful tool for many business and personal applications, I will be much less trusting of its output and take some time to verify before depending on it for a critical project or effort.

Familiarity Leading to Mistrust

It is unlikely that Alan Turing could have envisioned how his breakthrough research in the 1930s would evolve into modern AI. Merriam-Webster defines AI as "the capability of computer systems or algorithms to imitate intelligent human behavior."[153] This broad definition is quite appropriate as AI has evolved from theoretical concepts in the twentieth century to practical technologies today including self-driving cars, medical diagnostics, and voice assistants. The future uses for AI will likely transform how we live, work, and interact.

Not surprisingly, trust in AI is mixed and varies by region, application, and individual experience. In one of the largest global studies on AI, the University of Melbourne Business School in collaboration with KPMG surveyed over 48,000 people across forty-seven countries between November 2024 and January 2025 to find that less than half of global respondents are willing to trust it (46%).[154] This result was not confounded by the lack of familiarity with AI, as 66% of people surveyed were already intentionally using AI with some regularity. When compared to the last study of seventeen countries conducted by the same research group in 2022, it shows that people have become less trusting and more worried about AI as adoption has increased.

AI appears to be an outlier because most technological innovations, such as smartphones and computers, experience higher trust levels as usage and familiarity increase. According to the World Economic Forum, trust in AI is not accelerating as fast as the technology itself and lags past innovations.[155] This is a clear disconnect with other technologies and may limit its future use. It is not due to an understanding of the potential benefits of the technology as 83% of the people surveyed believe that AI will result in a wide range of benefits and 73% are already personally experiencing or observing benefits.[156]

Perhaps the counterintuitive results can be better explained by the environment. In the study, approximately three in five people within emerging economic countries trust AI systems, while in advanced economic countries approximately only two in five trust them. Specifically in the US, only 41% of the respondents were willing to trust AI. The country-by-country scores were almost inverted from the trust scores the people reported for their governments, with Scandinavian countries having the lowest scores for trust in AI. A hypothesis is that as people have lost trust in public officials, they are more willing to trust sources beyond public officials such as artificial intelligence. It could also be that the more you use AI, the more you discover its weaknesses.

The differences across countries continue to play out in terms of whether AI is worth the risk. Globally, 42% of people surveyed believe the benefits of AI outweigh the risks, compared to 32% who believe the risks outweigh the benefits, and 26% who believe benefits and risks are balanced. For more advanced economic countries, the benefit-to-risk ratio is much less positive with a third or less agreeing that the benefits outweigh the risks in Australia, New Zealand, the Netherlands, Sweden, Finland, Canada, Ireland, and France.

Also worth noting, the view that the benefits of AI outweigh the risks decreased from the 2022 study in which it stood at 50%. This reflected a decline across all but two of the seventeen countries in the study. As a result, we can conclude that people view the risks of AI as being higher as they become more aware of and familiar with its use.

To better understand the concern associated with AI use, the Pew Research Center surveyed over 5,000 Americans in June 2025 and found that the most common concern mentioned was about AI weakening human skills and connections.[157] Approximately half of the people reported that AI could erode creative thinking and want more control over its use.

Additional concerns include job displacement, loss of control over your life's decisions and actions, and ethical misuse. Respondents especially noted that they feel strongly that it's important to discern whether pictures, videos, or text were made by AI (as in deep fakes) or by humans. Unfortunately, people don't trust their own ability to spot AI-generated content, which creates further unease. With the rate of technological improvement, even experts may not be able to tell the difference in a few years.

There also exists a trust issue regarding AI producing accurate information. A study by Klaudia Jazwinska and Aisvarya Chandrasekar in March 2025 found that generative AI search tools not only fabricate citations but also undermine the flow of traffic to original publishers—an issue that carries serious implications for journalism and public trust in news.[158] The investigators further elaborated about hallucinations, the term for AI generating false information that "chatbots were generally bad at declining to answer questions they couldn't answer accurately, offering incorrect or speculative answers instead. Generative search tools often fabricated links and cited syndicated and copied versions of articles." The "I Don't Know" problem is significant as in tests with Gemini 3 Flash, the hallucination rate reached up to 91% in scenarios where the correct answer should be a refusal to answer.[159]

In 2025, average hallucination rates varied greatly across vendors ranging from 1% up to 58% for extremely complex data analysis. Still, Caltech researchers caution that AI is neither inherently trustworthy nor untrustworthy—its reliability depends on how it's trained, deployed, and monitored.[160] In order to make AI more trustworthy, government regulations are likely necessary. In late 2023, the European Union passed the world's first comprehensive legal framework for regulating artificial intelligence. AI governance continues to be a hot topic of ongoing policy discussion in the US and other countries. While some AI systems are regulated by individual agencies such as the FDA (Food and Drug Administration), no single US government agency has ownership of regulating AI, leaving it to companies and institutions to voluntarily adopt safeguards as they wish.

Certain business areas are of greater concern when using AI than others. In an article published in *The National Law Review* in 2025, three high-risk areas where you should be most cautious due to hallucination trends are legal and compliance, strategic finance and forecasting, and cybersecurity.[161] AI remains prone to "hallucinating" legal citations and misinterpreting complex regulatory language, showing error rates up to 34%, and resulting in several cases thrown out that otherwise had strong merit.

Concerning financial forecasts, roughly 18% of financial AI outputs have been flagged for providing deceptive or logically flawed projections, which can be disastrous for resource planning. Finally, in technical environments, AI can hallucinate the existence of non-existent security patches or "shadow libraries." As a result, a single hallucination regarding a system vulnerability or a maintenance threshold can lead to a catastrophic breach of the company's systems.

Besides improving the technology itself, key initiatives to improve the trustworthiness of AI include creating AI confidence indicators, which rate how certain an AI is about its answers, fact-checking integrations that link AI outputs to verified sources, and human-in-the-loop systems that combine AI with expert oversight.[162] Developers are also working to reduce the limitations and biases of the training data, which can skew the results produced by AI. These efforts are unlikely to be rolled out as quickly as AI technology advances, yet the magnitude of the adoption and utility of AI may be critical for AI to become a more trusted resource in society.

An unfortunate reality is that AI will likely develop a reputation for fabricating information before controls roll out, if it is even possible to develop such controls. Once mistrusted, it will be hard for AI to rebuild trust with many users as AI starts from an assumption of being factual, much like calculators; whereas, humans are known to have many flaws and are thereby forgiven for their warts. For my part, it will take a long time until I go on a new road trip in which I totally rely on AI for all my logistical planning.

The Bottom Line

AI has evolved from theoretical concepts to practical applications that can transform our daily lives across many dimensions. Surveys report that less than half of people around the world are willing to trust it, even though almost two-thirds use AI with some regularity. Unlike other recent technological innovations, trust in AI is going down as familiarity and usage increase. This is not the result of people not experiencing the benefits of AI but viewing the risks and potential misuse as growing in concern. This mistrust is strongest in countries with more advanced economies, including Scandinavia and the US. AI has also been shown to produce inaccurate and misleading information.

As a result of concerns relating to AI, people want more control over its use and to reserve its use. Government regulations have started to be enacted in different parts of the world, and several initiatives are underway by the industry to improve AI oversight, standards, and transparency. While these efforts should reduce the risks of AI and improve public perceptions of AI, the advances in technology will likely continue to outpace any corrective measures. Trust measures are expected to continue to erode until a more sustainable environment is established.

The So What

AI is supposed to revolutionize the way we live and work, and we are just beginning to realize its benefits. Even in advance of this realization, many organizational leaders are being asked to cut their budgets and head count due to the assumption that AI can replace or make workflows so much more efficient that fewer resources (employees) are needed to meet organizational objectives.

There's no doubt that there are many cases where this has already been realized in terms of administrative tasks and other repetitive, rule-based processes. For example, the Estee Lauder Companies utilize Google Cloud AI to allow brand leaders to generate various creative content, translate languages, and summarize meetings, enhancing productivity and customer experience. Verizon also uses Google AI tools to create, refine, and summarize emails and lengthy documents, and identify action items from email chains.[163] Yet we are truly at the beginning of this revolution, and its success is uncertain despite the enormous potential upside.

One of the biggest impediments to the implementation of AI is a lack of trust in technology. The trust issue is complex because it includes not understanding how the tech works, not believing in the results or output, and assuming that the technology may cause you as an employee to be no longer needed and therefore laid off. Each of these obstacles is challenging in their own right, yet collectively, if not overcome, will lead to at least a suboptimization of the potential of AI.

People are cautious of adopting new processes or technology in which they have very little idea as to how it works. While not a perfect analogy, even smartphones faced some challenges early on. Smartphones were not immediately adopted in the early 2000s partly due to unfamiliarity with how the technology worked and interfaced with other infrastructure, such as mobile coverage or slow internet. However, the integration of a phone and subsequently a camera within the smartphone created clear value and helped encourage even technically challenged consumers to try the device.

AI is much more complex to understand than smartphones, relying on machine learning, neural networks, and other computations to respond to searches or tasks. AI takes inputs and returns answers through algorithms that are hard to explain or comprehend. There aren't strong analogies for how and why it works, which makes it hard for people to apply prior knowledge. While the lower literacy–higher receptivity phenomenon, which supports that the less you know of something the more you may try it, may lead to initial use, adoption is unlikely to be sustainable without more understanding. Additionally, the technology has been used so broadly that defining its application sometimes can be difficult.

Perhaps more important for the optimal use of AI than knowing how it works is the obstacle of believing its results. In general, people tend to be skeptical of things that they do not understand and change that they do not wish to undertake. That skepticism can be further fueled by existing studies and viral examples of AI producing inaccurate information or inventing results. We have already discussed the problem of hallucination rates as high as 91%. For rates that high, there is ample reason for skepticism.

People, especially those who are resistant to change, are biased to overweight these extremes and begin questioning all the output from AI. Due to the complex nature of some of the tasks being requested of AI, verifying results to restore confidence can be challenging. The road map AI produced for my daughter's trip had many flaws, and it's made me more skeptical about relying on such plans more broadly.

The third major obstacle for trust in AI is simply fear, whether it is fear of AI replacing workers or that it will otherwise cause harm through unwanted surveillance, loss of autonomy, or obsolescence. Layoffs because of the implementation of AI are being realized and forecasted to accelerate across the economy, such that it is hard to escape the news on social and traditional media sources. Workers who feel vulnerable to being replaced by AI are unlikely to be supportive of adopting its use given the personal downside that would result.

Devious applications of AI, such as its use for covert influence and manipulation, cybercrime and espionage, and fraud and scams, also create warranted concern. Feeding into the fear and concern are iconic movies in which AI takes over the world including *The Matrix, The Terminator,* and *I, Robot.* All these factors create negative emotional energy for many people being asked to implement AI.[164]

As an organizational leader, you must take these obstacles into account when developing a plan for utilizing AI. You should be upfront and transparent about the plan, acknowledging that with any new technology there will be setbacks, yet explaining what the benefit is for the organization, its customers, and employees. With any change, certain groups are more likely to be early adopters due to their curiosity, technical proficiency, risk tolerance, and function.

The Trustworthy Decision Matrix can help you identify who should be included within the early trial for your company. Leaders should sequence AI trials such that the early learnings and bugs can be worked through by these early adopters, which creates some expertise and momentum for wider dissemination. A training program that educates and supports the AI rollout is also essential.

AI truly can be a game-changer over time for organizations, customers, and employees. Given its potential for creating value or disruption, leaders will need to guide their organizations to optimize its use in a thoughtful, proactive, and transparent manner. In addition to the usual challenges in implementing change, employees and organizational members may be biased to distrust AI, which places even greater importance on its rollout. Like almost every other human interaction, the sustainable adoption of AI will come down to whether AI proves trustworthy to its users. Your leadership challenge is to create the environment that makes that happen.

Winning Moves

Treat AI as a means to an end, and continually adjust its deployment in response to feedback, outcomes, and the level of trust it earns.

- ► Be sensitive to the distrust and fears that employees or members may have concerning AI and create a communication and support plan that directly addresses these concerns.

- Sequence the AI rollout to increase the likelihood of early wins and with initial users that are more inclined to trust and embrace the technology.
- Recognize that AI is a means to an end and that it is not a goal in itself.
- Continue to evaluate the use and rollout of AI to ensure its optimization.

13

THE ULTIMATE TRUST

I N July 2024, my father passed away from a heart attack. He was eighty-eight years old and had enjoyed a good life in which he had many great moments, a marriage of over fifty years, and three grandchildren. While he was taking medication for high blood pressure and experiencing normal signs of aging, he was generally in good health. So his sudden passing was quite unexpected.

My father had some notable accomplishments including saving the life of a complete stranger who had caught on fire while lighting a barbecue nearby us at a state park, being a pioneer in the advancement of color television technology, serving in the US Navy Reserve, and partnering with my mom to raise and provide for a family of two children. In his later years, my parents moved to be near my brother in Florida, and he remained committed to my mom despite her advanced Alzheimer's disease.

I remember when I received the call of his passing from my brother. Upon learning of such loss, I was surprised and quite sad as there was not going to be another opportunity to visit with him in this life. It may not have been comparable to the tragedy of losing a child or a loss of a loved one in the prime of their life, yet it was still a significant loss for my family and me.

There is no way to truly make sense of why someone dies and another lives. Some people attribute longevity to their good or bad deeds or some other convenient reason that helps justify their principles. As hard as it may be, I simply believe that there are events for which we never really know the true reason, but I have trust in G-d that it is part of his plan and am comforted by my absolute faith (as mentioned in the Introduction, a deep reverence and awe, grounded in Jewish law, strongly discourages writing the full name of the Divine, which is respected in this book).

For Those Who Have Faith

It would be incomplete and negligent to not discuss the influence of religion on trust in personal, professional, and societal settings. Before addressing trust from a religious perspective, it is important to level set on what is meant by faith. Trust and faith are so intertwined that the words are often used interchangeably even though they have different meanings. Faith is defined as a firm belief in something for which there is no proof and often refers to the trust in and loyalty to G-d.[165]

While faith and trust are often used interchangeably, the clearest difference between faith and trust is that faith may have no proven basis, and trust is typically a learned behavior that has some foundation in evidence or experience. Yet people can trust others without any reason as well. Perhaps more practically, faith is usually reserved for G-d or a religious context and trust for everything else. Many examples contradict these norms, but that should not be surprising for such broad terms.

The major world religions typically have trust in G-d as a core component of their faith, particularly in monotheistic faiths such as Judaism, Christianity, and Islam. A clear example comes from the learnings of the Lubavitcher Rebbe, Menachem Mendel Schneerson, which teach that trust applies to G-d and flows from faith, in which we not only have faith but also recognize that we rely on G-d for that which we need, certainly and constantly, without anxiety.[166] In Judeo-Christian beliefs, the first of the Ten Commandments is belief in the one and only G-d.[167] This commandment requires more than mere acknowledgment of G-d's existence; it demands an active, personal relationship characterized by faith, trust, and love.

As a very important concept relating to trust, many religions, including Christianity and Judaism, believe that G-d has a purposeful design for each individual and the world, even when the path is unclear or difficult to understand.[168] This divine plan may seem to conflict with the universal assumption of people's free will to choose their actions, whether for positive or negative reasons, although this is resolved in other teachings that are beyond the scope of this book.[169]

Trusting in G-d's plan means believing that there is a higher purpose behind everything, even when circumstances seem challenging or confusing. It requires acknowledging that a higher wisdom governs life's outcomes of which we are not capable of understanding. It does not mean that people are helpless or simply actors in a play, but that we may not be able to make sense out of some events that occur and that are ultimately for the good.

Trust in G-d or G-d's plan can create a positive attitude and provide emotional comfort.[170] Both religious teachings and scientific studies support the idea that such trust can help individuals manage difficult emotions and find peace.[171] Religious individuals may feel that life's events have meaning and purpose, which can help instill a general sense of trust in the world, reducing anxiety and fear. Studies suggest that individuals who strongly trust in G-d or a higher power often report feeling healthier. This is especially true within mental health research, which finds that trust in G-d correlates with lower levels of depression, stress, and anxiety, and with higher levels of happiness.[172] This is a relative and not an absolute measure, as there are many religious individuals with such problems.

Among the greatest coping tools in dealing with adversity is trust in G-d. People who rely on their relationship with G-d or their spiritual community often report greater resilience and well-being when facing hardship. This spiritual reliance can lead to personal growth and a deeper sense of peace. In a cross-sectional study of people affected by cancer, David Almaraz and colleagues analyzed the impact of the individual's relationship with G-d on the emotional health of people affected by cancer to find that trust in G-d and social support have a positive impact on the effective well-being of cancer patients, in contrast to mistrust in G-d.[173]

Many people trust religious institutions as pillars of moral authority and sources of social cohesion. A Pew Research Center study found that 89% of US adults believe religious institutions bring people together and strengthen community bonds.[174] Trust in these institutions can lead to greater engagement in community activities and reinforce religious identity. When religious institutions play a role in charitable work, education, or healthcare, they may be seen as more trustworthy. Studies indicate that religiously affiliated hospitals are perceived as more trustworthy and competent compared to their secular counterparts, with patients associating these institutions with higher warmth and ethical standards.[175]

In many contexts, trust in religious leaders is crucial. People often turn to religious figures for guidance on moral and ethical issues, and trust in these leaders can reinforce faith and adherence to religious teachings. Public perception of religious leaders' ethical standards plays a role in their overall trustworthiness. A survey by the Pew Research Center found that 65% of US adults believe religious leaders have high or very high ethical standards.[176] However, this perception varies among different religious affiliations and demographics.

Unfortunately, scandals or misconduct within religious institutions (I'm referring to cases of abuse and corruption) can significantly erode trust. Research has shown that in societies where trust in religious institutions declines, religious participation and engagement often decrease.[177] Similarly, data indicate that falling confidence in religious institutions is closely linked to declining religious affiliation and attendance. For example, the Catholic Church experienced a decline in institutional trust in certain regions due to revelations of abuse.[178] In 2017, nearly half of Catholics in the US (49%) told pollsters they had a "high" or "very high" opinion of the honesty and ethical standards of clergy members as conducted by a Gallup survey, yet just a year later after the abuse scandals were made public, that number had dropped to 31%.

Like secular social groups, trust levels can differ when comparing trust within religious groups versus among members of different religious groups. In some cases, individuals may have strong trust within their religious community but be more suspicious or distrustful of those outside it, especially in regions with interreligious conflict.[179] Studies have found that people who are religiously active tend to have higher levels of social trust, especially with others within their religious community.[180]

This is consistent with previous research that I have highlighted in which familiarity increases trust levels.

Being religious is not a significant factor in terms of being trustworthy in the broader population. Most Americans, 66% according to a Pew Research study in 2019, say religious and nonreligious people are equally trustworthy.[181] Prior to 2019, religious people were viewed to be more trustworthy, yet negative stories and scandals have also changed those scores. It is noteworthy that groups at the extreme ranges of religious identity feel differently. For example, evangelical Protestants are more likely to view religious people as more trustworthy, and atheists are more likely to view nonreligious people as more trustworthy.

Do religious people trust other institutions any more than nonreligious? Concerning science, there are substantial differences in levels of trust between religious and nonreligious groups. Jonathon McPhetres and Miron Zuckerman evaluated four relevant studies of over 9,000 people to find that general measures of religiosity are negatively associated with science knowledge.[182] More specifically, spiritual, Christian, and religious minority groups have shown lower trust in the scientific community compared to atheists and agnostics.

This issue came to a head during the COVID-19 pandemic in which trust in science and the COVID-19 vaccines differed across various groups. In an analysis by Emily Tippins and colleagues, vaccination intentions and trust in science varied as a function of religious group identity and beliefs.[183] Vaccine hesitancy was further linked to religiosity through a lack of trust in science. Even today, religious exemption is one of the greatest reasons cited for not receiving a vaccine.

Not surprisingly, highly religious individuals may place more trust in religious institutions than in secular ones, especially if they perceive the secular institutions to be corrupt or morally compromised. Conversely, in highly secular societies, religious institutions may be trusted less than government or scientific bodies.[184] These tendencies play out in communities and across countries and can be observed through voting blocks, response to regulations, and healthcare practices.

The role of religion in advancing trust can also vary significantly depending on the cultural and social context. In more religious societies, religious institutions and faith play a central role in building trust. By contrast, in secular societies, people may place greater trust in state institutions, scientific authorities, or secular moral frameworks. In societies undergoing secularization, the decline of religious authority can lead to shifts in where people place their trust. As religion plays a less dominant role in social life, other institutions, such as democratic governance or legal systems, may become the primary sources of trust.

The Bottom Line

Faith and trust are closely intertwined, with trust in G-d often flowing from a solid foundation of faith. Whether it is trust in G-d to provide for what is needed, the belief that there is divine purpose for each individual and the world, or that there is a divine plan that gives meaning to everything that happens, such trust in G-d allows people to better cope with events that may be tragic or that they do not understand. People who have trust in G-d also tend to have a positive outlook as they think about the unknown future, have better mental health, and may even experience improved health outcomes as evidenced in some small studies.

The association with religion does not necessarily lead to higher trust levels in many contexts. While it is true that many people trust religious institutions and their leaders, recent scandals have significantly reduced this level of trust. In recent years, people who are viewed as religious are not perceived as any more trustworthy than people who are not.

Evidence supports the idea that people who are religiously active tend to have higher levels of social trust, yet recent studies portray them as being less trusting of scientific information. Not surprisingly, those within religious environments are more trusting of each other than those who are outside of such environments and vice versa. This trust in those you know as opposed to those who you do not know remains consistent across almost all social dimensions.

The So What

It is challenging to write the practical takeaways for a chapter like this without sounding self-righteous or didactic, so I will simply note that those who have faith and trust in G-d find it helps them have a more positive outlook and better manage stress and disappointments. There are many other benefits and reasons to have faith and trust in G-d, yet these will be left to you to explore as you wish.

I believe that trust in G-d was not only important for the grieving process of my dad, but also dealing with other life challenges and uncertainty. Hopefully, you have either similar trust or other effective ways of managing unexpected life events.

Winning Moves

Assess your own beliefs to determine your faith in G-d to better explore your trust in G-d.

- ► To the degree that you trust in G-d, lean into that belief to improve your mental health and ability to cope with unforeseen events.
- ► Do not let your environment whether religious or secular dictate your trust in others or information.

14

MAKING TRUST YOUR COMPETITIVE ADVANTAGE

A FORMER COLLEAGUE OF MINE CALLED ME after a few years in which we had not spoken. After some small talk, Andrew said, "Michael, do you mind meeting with these people and see if it is worth your while? They seem like good guys that just need an 'in' to get their business going."

I replied, "If it passes your test, I am open to an introductory call to explore."

Via email, Andrew introduced me to two businessmen who were struggling to get access to companies that could import their product from Asia. The product was not overly exciting, but it was an incremental improvement over existing technology intended to support patients in self-monitoring their diabetes in South America. The technology was proven, and the sales pitch was clear and convincing. Yet after a year or so of trying to penetrate companies with various consultants and salespeople, they were unable to make any progress.

I did not have any technical skills that enabled me to better communicate the specifications of their technology. I also did not have expertise in import licenses from Asia to South America or the optimal process or logistics to make it happen. To make it even less compelling, I had limited time to devote to efforts that seemed like an unproductive diversion of my time and energy.

Still, they did need something that I could offer—the trust that I had built across industry professionals—in order to make some initial introductions to people that I knew or could get to. In return for such introductions, I would receive a sizable royalty stream on the revenues if the companies could ultimately agree upon a partnership. The time involved from me would be minimal as a few phone calls or emails could get the job done.

I thought about it, and the bigger issue for me concerning the opportunity was not the technology they had, but the businesspeople I was just introduced to. Were they credible enough to introduce them to the partners

I had worked with previously? In other words, could the introduction and subsequent business dealings harm the trust I had worked so hard to build with these foreign companies? As I was looking at the opportunity more optimistically, I considered that the introductions could prove to further those relationships by offering a new business opportunity and reinforcing a growing relationship with those companies. The decision for me was not truly about the amount of money that could be made or effort involved, but trust.

After some research, I decided to move forward and make the introductions. I knew two strong companies in South America that would likely have business interest in the technology and the ability to execute if their evaluation proved supportive to make a deal. It took me a few minutes to craft an email to one whom I had worked with a few years earlier on another venture. For the second company, I needed the help of another executive whom I knew but was too senior in their global organization to be directly involved. He gave me the contact within their South American subsidiary to help me, along with direction for them to prioritize my request.

I arranged the introductions, and both companies were supportive of conducting the product evaluations. The only reason that I could make those introductions was because I had developed trust with the key individuals years ago. The two businessmen were ecstatic as they had lived through years of promises and false hope in trying to have meetings with much lesser companies.

Whether the introductions eventually will lead to any income, it will take several months or even years to fully realize. Still, it is just one small instance of how trust can be the difference between success and failure, regardless of the assets or talents involved.

Unlocking Victory

Trust is a powerful catalyst for success—however you define it—both personally and professionally. Rarely will someone support a cause, political candidate, company, or colleague if some level of trust does not exist. It is the foundation for relationships whether with a friend, partner, peer, or boss. People seek out others whom they view as trustworthy, and social networks have been built around trust.[185]

It all starts with becoming trustworthy. That means being reliable, having integrity, being honest, having respect, being responsible, having empathy and caring, and being prone to guilt. You do not need to be perfect at all these attributes, yet consistency across the attributes and effort to improve will make up for occasional setbacks.

The first person who needs to be convinced that you are trustworthy is yourself. Self-trust empowers you to make decisions confidently, take calculated risks, and persist through setbacks. When you trust yourself, you are more likely to pursue your goals with determination and resilience. Not surprisingly, leaders who have greater self-trust tend to be trusted more by others.[186]

Once you have developed self-trust, the next step is to establish that same perception of trustworthiness with others. Only so much can be accomplished individually; success often depends on collaboration. Trust is essential for building meaningful relationships that allow you to go beyond yourself and accomplish something meaningful. You cannot assume that trust will be easily granted because real trust is often built gradually through consistent actions over time.

When you are trustworthy, others are more willing to support you, share information, and collaborate with you toward common goals. As depicted in the Trustworthy Decision Matrix, being trustworthy enables you to move forward on plans that you have proposed, whether easy or difficult in nature.

In leadership, trust is the basis for group cohesion and effectiveness. When people trust someone, they are more open to their ideas, more willing to follow their lead, and more likely to contribute their best efforts. Strong relationships based on trust facilitate better collaboration, more opportunities, and greater support networks. Trust also enables open communication, encourages innovation, and creates a psychologically safe environment where people feel comfortable sharing ideas and feedback.

In a highly effective organization or group, the leader uses trust to unleash the potential of its members and attract new members to the team. Trust becomes an important variable for leaders in making decisions on which projects should be supported and how resources are allocated, using the Trustworthy Decision Matrix or other tool.

When challenges arise, and they will, trust helps you navigate uncertainty. If you have self-trust, setbacks can be managed by relying on how you previously overcame similar obstacles, without panicking or giving up in the face of the obstacle. Trusting organizations are more likely to adapt, solve problems, and recover from setbacks due to a common belief in each other and ability to leverage each other's strengths. Trustworthy people are also more able to critically assess themselves, apologizing and correcting as needed, which can rebuild relationships after setbacks.

When you are trusted, people remember you and look forward to working with you again. I know this is the only reason that my former colleague reached out to me after several years and that I could do the same with people whom I had previously worked with. Being trustworthy is a strategic advantage and can be your most powerful catalyst for exceptional success.

The Bottom Line

Trust helps you succeed by empowering you to act confidently, supporting collaboration, strengthening relationships, and enabling effective leadership. By consistently demonstrating trustworthiness, you can build trust with yourself and others—laying the groundwork for long-term achievement and fulfillment. Trust is contagious as people who are trustworthy attract others who have similar values and behaviors. Whether in relation to a person, organization, or society at large, mastering the skills associated with trust will unlock countless dividends toward happiness, health, purpose, and wealth.

The So What

Having a reputation for being trustworthy opens up many opportunities, many of which will find you. People want to partner and work with others whom they can trust. Who would not prefer to work with someone you can count on versus someone you do not know or is untrustworthy? The Trustworthy Decision Matrix further validates this truism.

Trust is a force multiplier in building relationships and professional networks. A reputation of being trustworthy makes people willing to extend their own relationships to someone they have never met. The broader and deeper your professional network, the more likely you are to become aware of opportunities that circulate through trusted connections, not formal channels. A strong network helps leaders spot opportunities before competitors that could prove critical to business success or get early access to highly talented employees who are looking for other jobs due to an impending layoff.

While trustworthy people may be sought after by leaders or others to lead or work on projects, you can also proactively leverage the trust people have in you and your reputation to create new opportunities or steer situations in a preferred direction. For example, a leader with strong trust skills and a group of people with whom they have worked can seek introductions from their network to new customers or potential partners. These introductions could lead to sales or new business opportunities that significantly advance an organization. Someone who trusts another would see little downside in making the introduction, especially if they had made a similar introduction in the past.

Being proactive puts you in control. It empowers you to strategically create superior opportunities, moving beyond the limitations of merely evaluating existing choices that happen to find you. For example, a start-up company that does their homework to target and engage strategically aligned and well-resourced investors will be more successful in obtaining seed money than those who simply wait for private equity firms to find them. In talking to other companies about partnerships or deal making, taking the initiative may be the only way that other parties become aware of your openness and desire to partner.

For virtually any scenario, leaders who are proactive are better able to dictate the direction for their organization and create the ideal options for success compared to those who rely on incoming invitations.

Leaders who have a reputation for being trustworthy should therefore view their reputation as a competitive advantage that needs to be utilized like other assets of the organization. You should not be shy about asking for introductions or advice from people you trust. While asking for such support, you need to be prepared to reciprocate, consistent with trust-building behaviors. Leaders need to be careful regarding overextending their networks that may include people who are not trustworthy, which by association would begin eroding some of the trust capital that has been built. You need to be very protective of your reputation because once it is tarnished, it takes significant effort to rebuild.

Similar to external opportunities, leaders need to bring groups together within their organizations to pursue growth, resolve issues, and meet company targets. A leader who is willing to get directly involved in these pursuits can leverage their reputation for trust to create open channels for brainstorming, a safe environment to understand the root of key problems, and a cooperative environment in which people are willing to accept uncertainty or tradeoffs to meet their goals. For a leader not to put their reputation for trust on the line in these situations will almost guarantee failure from the lack of commitment of those involved. It is difficult to be a broker of a solution among groups if you don't extend your trust or are not viewed as trustworthy to begin with.

Whether for external or internal pursuits, being trustworthy will prove to increase the likelihood of success in almost any endeavor. Taking the initiative to use your reputation to inspire your team, solve key issues, and deliver results moves it from being a potential competitive advantage to one that is realized. That can be the pivotal factor that determines success or failure. It is only possible if you are trustworthy and are willing to treat trust as a competitive advantage for the challenge you are facing.

Winning Moves

Use the trust that you have to unlock new opportunities, solve problems, and elevate your leadership.

- ▶ Whether through self-trust or trust from others, don't let the fear of failure stand in your way to be all that you can be.
- ▶ Be proactive in deciding with whom and for what you are willing to extend trust.
- ▶ Share your knowledge of trust to help others achieve their goals.
- ▶ Leverage the trust you've built as a catalyst to expand your professional network.
- ▶ Don't be so protective of your reputation that you never use it as a competitive advantage.

NOTES

1   Merriam-Webster. (2024). Definition of trust. In *Merriam-Webster.com*. https://www.merriam-webster.com/dictionary/trust

2   Gottman, J. (2011, October 29). *John Gottman on trust and betrayal*. Greater Good. https://greatergood.berkeley.edu/article/item/john_gottman_on_trust_and_betrayal

3   Goldstein, S. (2025). Trust, safety, and control. *Psychology Today*. https://www.psychologytoday.com/us/blog/raising-resilient-children/202503/trust-safety-and-control

4   AlRuthia, Y., Sales, I., Almalag, H., Alwhaibi, M., Almosabhi, L., Albassam, A. A., Alharbi, F. A., Bashatah, A., & Asiri, Y. (2020). The relationship between health-related quality of life and trust in primary care physicians among patients with diabetes. *Clinical Epidemiology*, *12*, 143–151. https://doi.org/10.2147/CLEP.S236952

5   Acoba, E. F. (2024). Social support and mental health: The mediating role of perceived stress. *Frontiers in Psychology*, *15*(15), 1–12. https://doi.org/10.3389/fpsyg.2024.1330720

6   Gleeson, B. (2025, March 19). 5 proven ways trust is the ultimate competitive advantage. *Forbes*. https://www.forbes.com/sites/brentgleeson/2025/03/19/5-proven-ways-trust-is-the-ultimate-competitive-advantage/

7   Lilly, J. (1970). Psychological contract violation and the escalating cycle of mistrust. *Journal of Business Strategies*, *37*(1), 29–43. https://doi.org/10.54155/jbs.37.1.29-43

8   Gallup, Inc. (2013). *State of the American workplace.* Web. 21 June 2016.

9   Arrow, K. J. (1972). Gifts and exchanges. *Philosophy & Public Affairs 1*(4), 343–362. https://www.jstor.org/stable/2265097

10   Algan, Y., & Cahuc, P. (2013). Trust and growth. *Annual Review of Economics, 5*(1), 521–549. https://econpapers.repec.org/article/anrreveco/v_3a5_3ay_3a2013_3ap_3a521-549.htm

11   PwC. (2024, March 12). *Trust in US business survey.* https://www.pwc.com/us/en/library/trust-in-business-survey.html

12   Edelman. (2023). *Trust barometer special report—brand trust 2023.* https://www.edelman.com/trust/2023/trust-barometer/special-report-brand-trust

13   Deloitte Digital. *Trust ID.* https://www.deloittedigital.com/us/en/accelerators/trustid.html

14   Covey, S. M. R. (2007, June 4). *The business case for trust.* ChiefExecutive.net. https://chiefexecutive.net/the-business-case-for-trust/

15   CPABC's Professional Conduct Team. (2022, March 10). *Twenty years later: Lessons from Enron.* https://www.bccpa.ca/news-events/cpabc-newsroom/2022/march/twenty-years-later-lessons-from-enron/

16   Buffett, W. (2019). *"It takes 20 years to build a reputation and five minutes to ruin it. If you think about that you'll do things differently."* [Quote]. Goodreads.com. https://www.goodreads.com/quotes/148174-it-takes-20-years-to-build-a-reputation-and-five

17   Simpson, J. A., & Vieth, G. (2021). Trust and psychology: Psychological theories and principles underlying interpersonal trust. In F. Krueger (Ed.), *The neurobiology of trust* (pp. 15–35). Cambridge University Press. www.cambridge.org/core/books/abs/neurobiology-of-trust/trust-and-psychology/58784CAE33EBA214BEE047223DC69EBD

18   Severns, M. (2011, November 16). How do young children develop trust and distrust? *New America.* https://www.newamerica.org/early-elementary-education/early-ed-watch/how-do-young-children-develop-trust-and-distrust/

19 Betts, L. R., Rotenberg, K. J., & Trueman, M. (n.d.).
*Young children's interpersonal trust consistency as a predictor of
future school adjustment.* Retrieved April 18, 2025, from
https://irep.ntu.ac.uk/id/eprint/20050/1/215158_1125.pdf

20 Rotenberg, K. J., Addis, N., Betts, L. R., Corrigan, A., Fox, C.,
Hobson, Z., Rennison, S., Trueman, M., & Boulton, M. J. (2010).
The relation between trust beliefs and loneliness during early
childhood, middle childhood, and adulthood.
Personality and Social Psychology Bulletin, 36(8), 1086–1100.
https://doi.org/10.1177/0146167210374957

21 Malti, T., Averdijk, M., Zuffianò, A., Ribeaud, D., Betts,
L. R., Rotenberg, K. J., & Eisner, M. P. (2015). Children's trust and
the development of prosocial behavior.
International Journal of Behavioral Development, 40(3), 262-270.
https://doi.org/10.1177/0165025415584628
(Original work published 2016)

22 Rotenberg, K. J., Fox, C., Green, S., Ruderman, L., Slater, K.,
Stevens, K., & Carlo, G. (2005). *Construction and validation of
a children's interpersonal trust belief scale.* Faculty Publications,
Department of Psychology, University of Nebraska–Lincoln,
Digital Commons. https://digitalcommons.unl.edu/cgi/
viewcontent.cgi?article=1001&context=psychfacpub

23 Colì, E., Paciello, M., Lamponi, E., Calella, R., & Falcone, R.
(2023). Adolescents and trust in online social interactions:
A qualitative exploratory study. *Children, 10*(8), 1408.
https://doi.org/10.3390/children10081408

24 Flanagan, C. A., & Stout, M. (2010). Developmental patterns of
social trust between early and late adolescence: Age and school
climate effects. *Journal of Research on Adolescence, 20*(3),
748–773. https://doi.org/10.1111/j.1532-7795.2010.00658.x

25 Flanagan, C. A., & Stout, M. (2010). Developmental patterns of
social trust between early and late adolescence: Age and school
climate effects. *Journal of Research on Adolescence, 20*(3),
748–773. https://doi.org/10.1111/j.1532-7795.2010.00658.x

26 Evans, A. M., Dillon, K. D., Goldin, G., & Krueger, J. I. (2011).
Trust and self-control: The moderating role of the default.
Judgment and Decision Making, 6(7), 697–705.
https://doi.org/10.1017/S1930297500002709

27 Hancock, P. A., Kessler, T. T., Kaplan, A. D., Stowers, K., Brill, J. C., Billings, D. R., Schaefer, K. E., & Szalma, J. L. (2023). How and why humans trust: A meta-analysis and elaborated model. *Frontiers in Psychology, 14*(1), Article 1081086. https://doi.org/10.3389/fpsyg.2023.1081086

28 Segelken, H. R. (2014, May 20). Psychology study explains why strangers trust. *Cornell Chronicle.* https://news.cornell.edu/stories/2014/05/psychology-study-explains-why-strangers-trust

29 Freitag, M., & Bauer, Paul. C. (2016). Personality traits and the propensity to trust friends and strangers. *The Social Science Journal, 53*(4), 467–476. https://doi.org/10.1016/j.soscij.2015.12.002

30 Wurst, E. (2025, January 23). Tucson's Top Sports Stories: January 25. *Arizona Daily Star.* https://tucson.com/news/local/crime-courts/article_cb0149dc-d997-11ef-a466-c70904f6f3fd.html

31 New York University (2018, January 29). *Why do we trust, or not trust, strangers? The answer is Pavlovian, new psychology research finds* [News Release]. https://www.nyu.edu/about/news-publications/news/2018/january/why-do-we-trust--or-not-trust--strangers--the-answer-is-pavlovia.html

32 Ortiz-Ospina, E., Roser, M., & Arriagada, P. (2016, July). *Trust.* Our World in Data. ourworldindata.org/trust

33 American Diabetes Association. (2023, November 2). *Statistics about diabetes.* Diabetes.org. https://diabetes.org/about-diabetes/statistics/about-diabetes

34 Me-Kellams, C., & Lerner, J. S. (2016, April). *Trust your gut or think carefully? Examining whether an intuitive, versus a systematic, mode of thought produces greater empathic accuracy.* HKS Faculty Research Working Paper Series RWP16-017. Harvard Kennedy School. https://www.hks.harvard.edu/publications/trust-your-gut-or-think-carefully-examining-whether-intuitive-versus-systematic-mode

35 Ścigała, K. A., Schild, C., & Zettler, I. (2020). Dishonesty as a signal of trustworthiness: Honesty-Humility and trustworthy dishonesty. *Royal Society Open Science, 7*(10), 200685. https://doi.org/10.1098/rsos.200685

36 C.S. Lewis Foundation (n.d.). *Quotes misattributed to C.S. Lewis.* https://www.cslewis.org/aboutus/faq/quotes-misattributed/

37 Rotman, E. (2008). Therapeutic jurisprudence and terrorism. *SSRN Electronic Journal.* https://doi.org/10.2139/ssrn.1291868

38 UKEssays. (2018, November). *Analysis of public celebrity apologies in America.* https://www.ukessays.com/essays/media/analysis-public-celebrity-apologies-6727.php

39 Levine, E. (forthcoming). Who is trustworthy? Predicting trustworthy intentions and behavior. *Journal of Personality and Social Psychology.* Who-Is-Trustworthy-Predicting-Trustworthy-Intentions-and-Behavior.pdf

40 Walton, A. G. (2018, October 1). *People prone to feeling guilty are the most trustworthy.* The University of Chicago Booth School of Business. https://www.chicagobooth.edu/review/people-prone-feeling-guilty-are-most-trustworthy

41 Newrez. (2024, July 1). *Survey: When buyers seek a real estate agent, trust is essential.* https://www.newrez.com/blog/buying-selling/survey-when-buyers-seek-a-real-estate-agent-trust-is-essential/

42 Dhu, P. (2019, February 6). Consistency builds trust inconsistency breeds distrust. *Corporate Communication Experts.* corporatecommunicationexperts.com.au/consistency-builds-trust-inconsistency-breeds-distrust-by-peter-dhu/.

43 Wied, M., Koch-Ørvad, N., Welo, T., & Oehmen, J. (2020). Managing exploratory projects: A repertoire of approaches and their shared underpinnings. *International Journal of Project Management, 38*(2), 75–84. https://doi.org/10.1016/j.ijproman.2019.12.002

44 Nietzsche, F. (n.d.). *"I'm not upset that you lied to me, I'm upset that from now on I can't believe you."* [Quote]. Goodreads.com. https://www.goodreads.com/quotes/11864-i-m-not-upset-that-you-lied-to-me-i-m-upset

45 Wagner, M. L. (2000). *The power of apologies.* The Ombuds Office, University of Colorado, Boulder. https://hms.harvard.edu/sites/default/files/Departments/Ombuds%20Office/files/M.Wagner.ColumbiaUniversity.OmbudsOffice.ThePowerofApologies.pdf

46 Marino, M., Parrotta, P., Sala, D., & Valletta, G. (2024). The Volkswagen emissions scandal: Exploring the role of environmental concern and social norms. *Journal of Environmental Economics and Management, 127*(1), 103019. https://doi.org/10.1016/j.jeem.2024.103019

47 Cleveland Clinic. (2024, October 28). *How you can rebuild trust in any relationship*. https://health.clevelandclinic.org/how-to-rebuild-trust-in-a-relationship

48 Stein, J. (2011, December 8). *O.B.* Ultra tampons are coming back, and the company apologizes with a song. *Los Angeles Times.* https://www.latimes.com/health/la-xpm-2011-dec-08-la-heb-ob-tampons-return-20111208-story.html

49 Mayo Clinic Staff. (2022, November 22). *Forgiveness: Letting go of grudges and bitterness.* Mayo Clinic. https://www.mayoclinic.org/healthy-lifestyle/adult-health/in-depth/forgiveness/art-20047692

50 ADDO. (2020, April 14). *Why 86% of the couples rebuilding trust succeed in their relationship after a betrayal.* Addorecovery.com. https://www.addorecovery.com/rebuilding-trust-in-86-percent-of-relationships

51 Lewicki, R. J., Polin, B., & Lount, R. B. (2016). An exploration of the structure of effective apologies. *Negotiation and Conflict Management Research, 9*(2), 177–196. https://doi.org/10.1111/ncmr.12073

52 Hodgins, H. S., & Liebeskind, E. (2003). Apology versus defense: Antecedents and consequences. *Journal of Experimental Social Psychology, 39*(4), 297–316. https://doi.org/10.1016/s0022-1031(03)00024-6

53 Allan, A., de Mott, J., Larkins, I. M., Turnbull, L., Warwick, T., Willett, L., & Allan, M. M. (2022). The impact of voluntariness of apologies on victims' responses in restorative justice: Findings of a quantitative study. *Psychiatry, Psychology and Law, 29*(4), 593–609. https://doi.org/10.1080/13218719.2021.1956383

54 Scher, S. J., & Darley, J. M. (1997). How effective are the things people say to apologize? Effects of the realization of the apology speech act. *Journal of Psycholinguistic Research, 26*(1), 127–140. https://doi.org/10.1023/A:1025068306386

55 De Cremer, D., Pillutla, M. M., & Folmer, C. R. (2011). How important is an apology to you? Forecasting errors in evaluating the value of apologies. *Psychological Science, 22*(1), 45–48. https://doi.org/10.1177/0956797610391101

56 US Department of Justice (21 February 2020). Wells Fargo Agrees to Pay $3 Billion to Resolve Criminal and Civil Investigations into Sales Practices. https://www.justice.gov/archives/opa/pr/wells-fargo-agrees-pay-3-billion-resolve-criminal-and-civil-investigations-sales-practices

57 Fehr, R., Gelfand, M. J., & Nag, M. (2010). The road to forgiveness: A meta-analytic synthesis of its situational and dispositional correlates. *SSRN Electronic Journal.* https://doi.org/10.2139/ssrn.1612494

58 Beyens, U., Yu, H., Han, T., Zhang, L., & Zhou, X. (2015). The strength of a remorseful heart: Psychological and neural basis of how apology emolliates reactive aggression and promotes forgiveness. *Frontiers in Psychology, 6,* 1611. https://doi.org/10.3389/fpsyg.2015.01611

59 Maddux, W. W., Kim, P. H., Okumura, T., & Brett, J. M. (2011). Cultural differences in the function and meaning of apologies. *International Negotiation, 16*(3), 405–425. https://doi.org/10.1163/157180611x592932

60 Smith, A. K., Bolton, R. N., & Wagner, J. (1999). A model of customer satisfaction with service encounters involving failure and recovery. *Journal of Marketing Research, 36*(3), 356–372. https://doi.org/10.1177/002224379903600305

61 Kim, P. H., Ferrin, D. L., Cooper, C. D., & Dirks, K. T. (2004). Removing the shadow of suspicion: The effects of apology versus denial for repairing competence- versus integrity-based trust violations. *Journal of Applied Psychology* 89(1):104–118.

62 Bajarin, T. (2015, June 30). How Taylor Swift Saved Apple Music. *Time.* https://time.com/3940500/apple-music-taylor-swift-release/

63 University of Cambridge Judge Business School. (2014, December 16). *The art of apologising.* https://www.jbs.cam.ac.uk/2014/the-art-of-apologising/competence- versus integrity-based trust

violations. *Journal of Applied Psychology, 89*(1), 104–118. https://doi.org/10.1037/0021-9010.89.1.104

64   Reuters 2 June 2010). BP CEO apologizes for thoughtless oil spill comment. https://www.reuters.com/article/business/environment/bp-ceo-apologizes-for-thoughtless-oil-spill-comment-idUSTRE6515NQ/

65   Lee, W. S., & Selart, M. (2015). How betrayal affects emotions and subsequent trust. *The Open Psychology Journal, 8*(1), 153–159. https://doi.org/10.2174/1874350101508010153

66   Fortune Business Insights. (n.d.). *Corporate leadership training market size, share & industry analysis, by end-user, application, and regional forecast, 2024–2032.* https://www.fortunebusinessinsights.com/corporate-leadership-training-market-108699

67   PwC. (2024, March 12). *Trust in US business survey.* https://www.pwc.com/us/en/library/trust-in-business-survey.html

68   PwC. (2024, July 22). *How to earn customer trust in your sector.* www.pwc.com/us/en/library/trust-in-business-survey/customer-trust-in-your-sector.html

69   Frydlinger, D., Cummins, T., Vitasek, K., & Bergman, J. (n.d.). *Unpacking relational contracts: The practitioner's go-to guide for understanding relational contracts.* IACCM. https://www.worldcc.com/Portals/IACCM/resources/files/9487_unpacking-relational-con-tractingv19-oct-11-2016.pdf

70   Stuckey, J., & White, D. (1993, August 1). *When and when not to vertically integrate.* McKinsey & Company. https://www.mckinsey.com/capabilities/strategy-and-corporate-finance/our-insights/when-and-when-not-to-vertically-integrate

71   Zak, P. J. (2017, January-February). The neuroscience of trust. *Harvard Business Review.* https://hbr.org/2017/01/the-neuroscience-of-trust

72   Vorecol Editorial Team. (2024, November 13). How does trust influence employee retention rates in organizations? Exploring the correlation. *Vorecol.com.* https://vorecol.com/blogs/blog-how-does-trust-influence-employee-retention-rates-in-organizations-exploring-the-correlation-208072

73 Borkowski, C., & Kaynas, R. (2025, March 25). *Telework trends.* Bureau of Labor Statistics. https://www.bls.gov/opub/btn/ volume-14/telework-trends.htm

74 Expert Panel. (2024, January 30). Council post: 20 tips for mastering the art of remote work management. *Forbes.* https://www.forbes.com/councils/forbeshumanresourcescouncil/ 2024/01/30/20-tips-for-mastering-the-art-of-remote-work-man- agement/

75 Thiel, C., Bonner, J. M., Bush, J., Welsh, D., & Garud, N. (2022, June 27). Monitoring employees makes them more likely to break rules. *Harvard Business Review.* https://hbr.org/2022/06/ monitoring-employees-makes-them-more-likely-to-break-rules

76 PSHRA. (2024, July). *Losing faith: New report finds public trust in government on the wane.* https://pshra.org/losing-faith-new- report-finds-public-trust-in-government-on-the-wane/

77 OECD. (2024, July 10). *OECD survey on drivers of trust in public institutions 2024 results—country notes: Canada.* https://www.oecd.org/en/publications/oecd-survey-on- drivers-of-trust-in-public-institutions-2024-results-country- notes_a8004759-en/canada_1d3c42d0-en.html

78 Clausen, B., Kraay, A., & Nyiri, Z. (2011). Corruption and confidence in public institutions: Evidence from a global survey. *The World Bank Economic Review, 25*(2), 212–249. https://doi.org/10.1093/wber/lhr018

79 Rastogi, A., Pati, S. P., Krishnan, T. N., & Krishnan, S. (2018). Causes, contingencies, and consequences of disengagement at work: An integrative literature review. *Human Resource Development Review, 17*(1), 62–94. https://doi.org/10.1177/1534484317754160

80 *Britannica Money.* (2024, July 17). *Consumer Financial Protection Bureau.* https://www.britannica.com/money/ Consumer-Financial-Protection-Bureau

81 Sharma, K., Schoorman, F. D., & Ballinger, G. A. (2022). How can it be made right again? A review of trust repair research. *Journal of Management, 49*(1), 363–399. https://doi.org/10.1177/01492063221089897

82 McKenzie, W. (2023). Restoring trust in the media. *The Catalyst, 28*. George W. Bush Institute. https://www.bushcenter.org/catalyst/the-fix/restoring-trust-in-the-media

83 Pew Research Center. (2025, December 4). *Public trust in government: 1958–2024.* www.pewresearch.org/politics/2024/06/24/public-trust-in-government-1958-2024/.

84 Barthel, M. L., & Moy, P. (2015). The media and the fostering of political (dis)trust. In K. Kenski, & K. H. Jamieson (Eds.), *The Oxford Handbook of Political Communication* (pp. 581–594). Oxford University Press. https://doi.org/10.1093/oxfordhb/9780199793471.013.51

85 Jurkowitz, M., Mitchell, A., Shearer, E., & Walker, M. (2020, January 24). *U.S. Media polarization and the 2020 election: A nation divided.* Pew Research Center. https://www.pewresearch.org/journalism/2020/01/24/u-s-media-polarization-and-the-2020-election-a-nation-divided/

86 Brenan, M., & Saad, L. (2025, February 27). *Five key insights into Americans' views of the news media.* Gallup. https://news.gallup.com/opinion/gallup/657239/five-key-insights-americans-views-news-media.aspx

87 Ognyanova, K., Lazer, D., Robertson, R. E., & Wilson, C. (2020). Misinformation in action: Fake news exposure is linked to lower trust in media, higher trust in government when your side is in power. *Harvard Kennedy School Misinformation Review, 1*(4). https://doi.org/10.37016/mr-2020-024

88 Adams, Z., Osman, M., Bechlivanidis, C., & Meder, B. (2023). (Why) is misinformation a problem? *Perspectives on Psychological Science, 18*(6), 1436–1463. https://doi.org/10.1177/17456916221141344

89 St. Aubin, C., & Liedke, J. (2025, September 25). *Social media and news fact sheet.* Pew Research Center. https://www.pewresearch.org/journalism/fact-sheet/social-media-and-news-fact-sheet/

90 Scartascini, C. (2021, October 6). Testing the impact of social media on trust. *IDB.* https://www.iadb.org/en/blog/research-development/testing-impact-social-media-trust

91   Ancona, L., Karl, G., Martì, A., & Samek, W. (2023, April).
     Has the time come to end anonymity on social media? *SciencesPo.*
     https://www.sciencespo.fr/public/chaire-numerique/wp-content/
     uploads/2023/07/VO-Anonymity.pdf

92   Cinelli, M., Morales, G. D. F., Galeazzi, A., Quattrociocchi, W.,
     & Starnini, M. (2021). The echo chamber effect on social media.
     Proceedings of the National Academy of Sciences U.S.A., 118(9),
     Article e2023301118. https://doi.org/10.1073/pnas.2023301118

93   Putri, S. D. G., Purnomo, E. P., & Khairunissa, T. (2024). Echo
     chambers and algorithmic bias: The homogenization of online
     culture in a smart society. *SHS Web of Conferences, 202,* Article
     05001. https://doi.org/10.1051/shsconf/202420205001

94   St. Aubin, C., & Liedke, J. (2025, September 25). *Social media and
     news fact sheet.* Pew Research Center. https://www.pewresearch.
     org/journalism/fact-sheet/social-media-and-news-fact-sheet/

95   Pew Research Center. (2019, July 22). *Trust and distrust in
     America: The state of personal trust.* https://www.pewresearch.
     org/politics/2019/07/22/the-state-of-personal-trust/

96   Knight Foundation. (n.d.). *Perceived accuracy and bias in the
     news media: A Gallup/Knight Foundation survey.*
     https://knightfoundation.org/wp-content/uploads/2020/03/
     KnightFoundation_AccuracyandBias_Report_FINAL.pdf

97   Edelman. (2025). *Global report: Trust and the crisis of grievance.*
     https://www.edelman.com/sites/g/files/aatuss191/files/
     2025-01/2025%20Edelman%20Trust%20Barometer%20
     Global%20Report_01.23.25.pdf

98   Brenan, M. (2024, October 14). *Americans' trust in media remains
     at trend low.* Gallup. https://news.gallup.com/poll/651977/
     americans-trust-media-remains-trend-low.aspx

99   Edelman. (2025). *Global report: Trust and the crisis of grievance.*
     https://www.edelman.com/sites/g/files/aatuss191/files/
     2025-01/2025%20Edelman%20Trust%20Barometer%20
     Global%20Report_01.23.25.pdf

100 Neureiter, A., Stubenvoll, M., Kaskeleviciute, R., & Matthes, J. (2021). Trust in Science, Perceived Media Exaggeration About COVID-19, and Social Distancing Behavior. *Frontiers in Public Health, 9,* Article 670485. https://doi.org/10.3389/fpubh.2021.670485

101 *Special Report: Trust and Health.* (n.d.). https://www.edelman.com/trust/2024/trust-barometer/special-report-health

102 Deloitte. (2025, March 25). *2025 digital media trends: Social platforms are becoming a dominant force in media and entertainment.* https://www2.deloitte.com/us/en/insights/industry/technology/digital-media-trends-consumption-habits-survey/2025.html

103 Kivak, R. (2025). *Citizen journalism.* EBSCO Information Services, Inc. https://www.ebsco.com/research-starters/communication-and-mass-media/citizen-journalism

104 Stocking, G., Wang, L., Lipka, M., Matsa, K. E., Widjaya, R., Tomasik, E., & Liedke, J. (2024, November 18). *America's news influencers.* Pew Research Center. https://www.pewresearch.org/journalism/2024/11/18/americas-news-influencers/

105 Lord, K., M., & Vogt, K. (2021, March 18). *Strengthen media literacy to win the fight against misinformation.* Stanford Social Innovation Review. https://ssir.org/articles/entry/strengthen_media_literacy_to_win_the_fight_against_misinformation

106 Altay, S., De Angelis, A., & Hoes, E. (2024). Media literacy tips promoting reliable news improve discernment and enhance trust in traditional media. *Communications Psychology, 2,* Article 74. https://doi.org/10.1038/s44271-024-00121-5

107 Gibson, H., Kirkconnell-Kawana, L., & Proctor, E. (2022, November). *News literacy report: Lessons in building public confidence and trust.* Impress. https://i.emlfiles4.com/cmpdoc/8/7/2/0/4/3/files/7583_impress-news-literacy-report-1.pdf?dm_i=7AK6

108 Hutton, Z. (2023, November 16). States begin to address media literacy through legislation. *Governing.* www.governing.com/education/states-begin-to-address-media-literacy-through-legislation

109 Kožuh, I., & Čakš, P. (2023). Social media fact-checking: The effects of news literacy and news trust on the intent to verify health-related information. *Healthcare, 11*(20), 2796. https://doi.org/10.3390/healthcare11202796

110 Schwartz, J. (2017, December 13). *The New York Times* D.C. bureau adds fact-checker. *Politico.* https://www.politico.com/story/2017/12/13/new-york-times-fact-checker-295403

111 Fischer, S. (2025, April 22). *Axios Media Trends.* Axios. https://www.axios.com/newsletters/axios-media-trends-a189b090-1ed8-11f0-9620-25e6c4b430eb.html?utm_source=newsletter&utm_medium=email&utm_campaign=newsletter_axiosmediatrends&stream=top

112 Bachmann, I., & Valenzuela, S. (2023). Studying the downstream effects of fact-checking on social media: Experiments on correction formats, belief accuracy, and media trust. *Social Media + Society, 9*(2). https://doi.org/10.1177/20563051231179694

113 *Axios.* (2025). Axios. https://www.axios.com/newsletters/axios-media-trends-a189b090-1ed8-11f0-9620-25e6c4b430eb.html?utm_source=newsletter&utm_medium=email&utm_campaign=newsletter_axiosmediatrends&stream=top

114 Miller, M. (2025, April 16). *State Department eliminates key office tasked with fighting foreign disinformation.* Politico. https://www.politico.com/news/2025/04/16/state-department-shutters-gec-foreign-disinformation-00292982

115 Waxman, O. B. (2014, April 30). What's really in Taco Bell beef. *Time.* https://time.com/83184/whats-really-in-taco-bell-beef/)

116 Taylor, K. (2019, June 25). Wayfair Furniture Employees Walked Out Over Sales to Migrant Facilities. *The New York Times.* https://www.nytimes.com/2019/06/25/us/wayfair-walkout.html

117 Fennell, S. (2024, August 26). *The connection between self-trust and self-esteem: Building a solid foundation for well-being.* Riviera Therapy. https://rivieratherapy.com/the-connection-between-self-trust-and-self-esteem-building-a-solid-foundation-for-well-being/

118 Bloom, L., & Bloom, C. (2019, September 12). Self-Trust and how to build it. *Psychology Today*. https://www.psychologytoday.com/us/blog/stronger-the-broken-places/201909/self-trust-and-how-build-it

119 NHS. (2023, April 11). *Raising low self-esteem.* https://www.nhs.uk/mental-health/self-help/tips-and-support/raise-low-self-esteem/

120 Markway, B. (2018, September 20). Why self-confidence is more important than you think. *Psychology Today.* https://www.psychologytoday.com/us/blog/shyness-is-nice/201809/why-self-confidence-is-more-important-you-think

121 DeBord, K. (2001, March 1). *Self-Esteem in children.* NC State Extension Publications. https://content.ces.ncsu.edu/self-esteem-in-children

122 Ilies, R., De Pater, I., & Judge, T. (2007). Differential affective reactions to negative and positive feedback, and the role of self-esteem. *Journal of Managerial Psychology, 22*(6), 590–609. https://doi.org/10.1108/02683940710778459

123 Kim, J., Kwon, J. H., Kim, J., Kim, E. J., Kim, H. E., Kyeong, S., & Kim, J.-J. (2021). The effects of positive or negative self-talk on the alteration of brain functional connectivity by performing cognitive tasks. *Scientific Reports, 11*, Article 14873. https://doi.org/10.1038/s41598-021-94328-9

124 Mayo Clinic. (2023, November 21). *Positive thinking: Stop negative self-talk to reduce stress.* https://www.mayoclinic.org/healthy-lifestyle/stress-management/in-depth/positive-thinking/art-20043950

125 Crosswell, A. D., Moreno, P. I., Raposa, E. B., Motivala, S. J., Stanton, A. L., Ganz, P. A., & Bower, J. E. (2017). Effects of mindfulness training on emotional and physiologic recovery from induced negative affect. *Psychoneuroendocrinology, 86*, 78–86. https://doi.org/10.1016/j.psyneuen.2017.08.003

126 Pennebaker, J. W. (2017). Expressive writing in psychological science. *Perspectives on Psychological Science, 13*(2), 226–229. https://doi.org/10.1177/1745691617707315

127 Minichiello, H., Reasonover, M., & Fuglestad, P. (2024). The indirect effects of perfectionism on athletes' self-views through maladaptive emotion regulation. *Frontiers in Psychology*, *15*, Article 1373461. https://doi.org/10.3389/fpsyg.2024.1373461

128 Cleveland Clinic. (2021, October 22). *Atelophobia (Fear of Imperfection)*. https://my.clevelandclinic.org/health/diseases/21932-atelophobia-fear-of-imperfection

129 Key, K. (2021, March 29). Overcoming fear of making mistakes. *Psychology Today*. https://www.psychologytoday.com/us/blog/counseling-keys/202103/overcoming-fear-of-making-mistakes

130 De Leersnyder, J., Boiger, M., & Mesquita, B. (2013). Cultural regulation of emotion: Individual, relational, and structural sources. *Frontiers in Psychology*, *4*(55), 1–11. https://doi.org/10.3389/fpsyg.2013.00055

131 Mui, C. (2012). How Kodak failed. *Forbes*. https://www.forbes.com/sites/chunkamui/2012/01/18/how-kodak-failed/

132 Deane, C. (2024, October 17). *Americans' deepening mistrust of institutions*. The Pew Charitable Trusts. https://www.pewtrusts.org/en/trend/archive/fall-2024/americans-deepening-mistrust-of-institutions

133 Pollard, M. S., & Davis, L. M. (2022). Decline in trust in the Centers for Disease Control and Prevention during the COVID-19 pandemic. *Rand Health Quarterly*, *9*(3), 23. https://pmc.ncbi.nlm.nih.gov/articles/PMC9242572/

134 Suhay, E., Soni, A., Persico, C., & Marcotte, D. E. (2022). Americans' trust in government and health behaviors during the COVID-19 pandemic. *RSF: The Russell Sage Foundation Journal of the Social Sciences*, *8*(8), 221–244. https://doi.org/10.7758/RSF.2022.8.8.10

135 Aassve, A., Capezzone, T., Cavalli, N., Conzo, P., & Peng, C. (2024). Social and political trust diverge during a crisis. *Scientific Reports*, *14*, Article 331. https://doi.org/10.1038/s41598-023-50898-4

136 Perlis, R. H., Ognyanova, K., Uslu, A., Trujillo, K. L., Santillana, M., Druckman, J. N., Baum, M. A., & Lazer, D. (2024). Trust in physicians and hospitals during the COVID-19 pandemic in a 50-state survey of US adults. *JAMA Network Open, 7*(7): Article e2424984. https://doi.org/10.1001/jamanetworkopen.2024.24984

137 Arnstein Aassve, et al. "Social and Political Trust Diverge during a Crisis." *Scientific Reports*, vol. 14, no. 1, 3 Jan. 2024, https://doi.org/10.1038/s41598-023-50898-4.

138 Nguyen, H. (2022, June 15). *The Reuters Institute releases 11th edition of the world's largest digital news report.* Yougov.com. https://business.yougov.com/content/ 42833-reuters-institute-digital-news-report-2022-yougov

139 USC Shoah Foundation. (2010). *Genocide Against the Tutsi in Rwanda*. USC Shoah Foundation. https://sfi.usc.edu/collections/ rwandan

140 Edelman. (2023). *2023 Edelman Trust Barometer.* https://www.edelman.com/trust/2023/trust-barometer

141 Lee, A. H.-Y. (2022). Social trust in polarized times: How perceptions of political polarization affect Americans' trust in each other. *Political Behavior, 44*(3), 1533–1554. https://doi.org/10.1007/s11109-022-09787-1

142 Doherty, C. (n.d.). *FOR RELEASE JUNE 24, 2024 FOR MEDIA OR OTHER INQUIRIES.* https://www.pewresearch.org/ wp-content/uploads/sites/20/2024/06/PP_2024.6.24_role-of- government_REPORT.pdf

143 Edelman. (2024). *Global Report*. Edelman Trust Institute. (2024). *2024 Edelman Trust Barometer Global Report.* https://www.edelman.com/sites/g/files/aatuss191/files/ 2024-02/2024%20Edelman%20Trust%20Barometer%20 Global%20Report_FINAL.pdf

144 Roth, F. (2009). The effect of the financial crisis on systemic trust. *Intereconomics, 44*(4), 203–208. https://doi.org/10.1007/ s10272-009-0296-9

145 E-Poll Market Research Blog. (2025, February 24). *Which technology companies do consumers trust?* https://blog.epollresearch.com/2025/02/24/ which-technology-companies-do-consumers-trust/

146 *A-41. People at work by telework status and selected characteristics.* (2025, September 5). Bureau of Labor Statistics. https://www.bls.gov/web/empsit/cpseea41.htm

147 Pabilonia, S. W., & Redmond, J. J. (2024, October). The rise in remote work since the pandemic and its impact on productivity. *Beyond the Numbers: Productivity 13*(8). US Bureau of Labor Statistics. https://www.bls.gov/opub/btn/volume-13/remote-work-productivity.htm

148 Stavrova, O., Spiridonova, T., van de Calseyde, P., Meyers, C., & Evans, A. M. (2023). Does remote work erode trust in organizations? A within-person investigation in the COVID-19 context. *Social and Personality Psychology Compass, 17*(7): Article e12762. https://doi.org/10.1111/spc3.12762

149 World Values Survey. (2022). *World Values Survey Wave 7 (2017-2022).* www.worldvaluessurvey.org/WVSDocumentationWV7.jsp.

150 Edelman. (2022). *2022 Edelman Trust Barometer.* www.edelman.com/trust/2022-trust-barometer.

151 Weining, A. N., & Smith, E. L. (2012). Self-Esteem and trust: Correlation between self-esteem and willingness to trust in undergraduate students. *Inquiries Journal,* 4(08). http://www.inquiriesjournal.com/articles/688/self-esteem-and-trust-correlation-between-self-esteem-and-willingness-to-trust-in-undergraduate-students

152 Kyle DeMaria (ed.), Page, I., Reuss, K., & Zemper, Z. (2024, August). Changes in the US Labor Supply. *Trendlines*, US Department of Labor, Employment and Training Administration. https://www.dol.gov/sites/dolgov/files/ETA/opder/DASP/Trendlines/posts/2024_08/Trendlines_August_2024.html

153 Merriam-Webster. (n.d.). Definition of artificial intelligence. In Merriam-Webster.com. https://www.merriam-webster.com/dictionary/artificial%20intelligence

154 Gillespie, N., Lockey, S., Ward, T., Macdade, A., & Hassed, G. (2025). Trust, attitudes and use of artificial intelligence: A global study 2025. *The University of Melbourne and KPMG.* https://doi.org/10.26188/28822919

155 Elliott, D. (2024, February 13). *Don't trust technology and AI? This expert explains why.* World Economic Forum. https://www.weforum.org/stories/2024/02/trust-technology-ai-citizen-participation/

156 Trust, attitudes and use of artificial intelligence A global study 2025. (n.d.). https://doi.org/10.26188/28822919

157 Kennedy, B.,Yam, E., Kikuchi, E., Pula, I., & Fuentes, J. (2025, September 17). *How Americans view AI and its impact on people and society.* Pew Research Center. https://www.pewresearch.org/science/2025/09/17/how-americans-view-ai-and-its-impact-on-people-and-society/

158 Jazwinska, K., & Chandrasekar, A. (2025, March 6). AI search has a citation problem. *Columbia Journalism Review.* https://www.cjr.org/tow_center/we-compared-eight-ai-search-engines-theyre-all-bad-at-citing-news.php

159 Schwartz, E. H. (2025, December 22). *Gemini 3 Flash is smart — but when it doesn't know, it makes stuff up anyway.* TechRadar. https://www.techradar.com/ai-platforms-assistants/gemini-3-flash-is-smart-but-when-it-doesnt-know-it-makes-stuff-up-anyway

160 CalTech. (n.d.). *Can we trust artificial intelligence?* Caltech Science Exchange. https://scienceexchange.caltech.edu/topics/artificial-intelligence-research/trustworthy-ai

161 Howell, C. T. (2025). AI Hallucinations are Creating Real-World Risks for Businesses. *The National Law Review.* https://natlawreview.com/article/ai-hallucinations-are-creating-real-world-risks-businesses

162 Jacovi, A., Wang, A., Alberti, C., Tao, C., Lipovetz, J., Olszewska, K., Haas, L., Liu, M., Keating, N., Bloniarz, A., Saroufim, C., Fry, C., Kukliansky, D., Singh Tomar, G., Swirhun, J., Xing, J., Wang, L., Gurumurthy, M., … Das, D. (2024, December 17). *The FACTS Grounding Leaderboard: Benchmarking LLMs' ability to ground responses to long-form input.* Google. https://storage.googleapis.com/deepmind-media/FACTS/FACTS_grounding_paper.pdf

163 Hall, B. (2024, April 12). *101 real-world gen AI use cases from the world's leading organizations*. Google Cloud Blog. https://cloud.google.com/transform/101-real-world-generative-ai-use-cases-from-industry-leaders

164 Sieja, Z. (2025, October 15). *Top 15 artificial intelligence movies and TV series to watch in 2025*. DLabs.AI. https://dlabs.ai/blog/top-artificial-intelligence-movies-and-tv-series/

165 Merriam-Webster. (n.d.). Definition of faith. In Merriam-Webster. com. https://www.merriam-webster.com/dictionary/faith

166 The Rebbe.org. (n.d.). *Faith and trust*. Chabad.org. https://www.chabad.org/therebbe/article_cdo/aid/2296503/jewish/Faith-and-Trust.htm

167 Tauber, Y. (n.d.). *The first commandment*. Chabad.org. https://www.chabad.org/library/article_cdo/aid/2917/jewish/The-First-Commandment.htm

168 *Topical Bible: Divine Design and Purpose*. (n.d.). Biblehub.com. https://biblehub.com/topical/d/divine_design_and_purpose.htm

169 Freeman, T. (n.d.). *Can my free will mess up G-d's plans? - All the responsibility, no room for despair*. Chabad.org. https://www.chabad.org/library/article_cdo/aid/3928230/jewish/Free-Will-and-G-ds-Plans.htm

170 Kent, B. V., Bradshaw, M., & Uecker, J. E. (2017). Forgiveness, attachment to God, and mental health outcomes in older U.S. adults: A longitudinal study. *Research on Aging, 40*(5), 456–479. https://doi.org/10.1177/0164027517706984

171 Rosmarin, D. H., Pargament, K. I., & Mahoney, A. (2009). The role of religiousness in anxiety, depression, and happiness in a Jewish community sample: A preliminary investigation. *Mental Health, Religion & Culture, 12*(2), 97–113. https://doi.org/10.1080/13674670802321933

172 Zhu, X., & Upenieks, L. (2022). Age differences in mental health during the COVID-19 pandemic: Assessing the moderating role of attachment to God. *Journal of Aging and Health, 35*(9), 607–622. https://doi.org/10.1177/08982643221112141

173 Almaraz, D., Saiz, J., Moreno Martín, F., Sánchez-Iglesias, I., Molina, A. J., Goldsby, T. L., & Rosmarin, D. H. (2022). Religiosity, emotions and health: The role of trust/mistrust in God in people affected by cancer. *Healthcare, 10*(6), 1138. https://doi.org/10.3390/healthcare10061138

174 Pew Research Center. (2025). *2023-24 US Religious Landscape Study Interactive Database.* Pew Research Center's Religion & Public Life Project. https://www.pewresearch.org/religious-landscape-study/

175 Seemann, A.-K., Drevs, F., Gebele, C., & Tscheulin, D. K. (2015). Are religiously affiliated hospitals more than just nonprofits? A study on stereotypical patient perceptions and preferences. *Journal of Religion and Health, 54*(3), 1027–1039. https://doi.org/10.1007/s10943-014-9880-9

176 Pew Research Center. (2019, November 15). *Most congregants trust clergy to give advice about religious issues, fewer trust clergy on personal matters.* Pew Research Center's Religion & Public Life Project. https://www.pewresearch.org/religion/2019/11/15/most-congregants-trust-clergy-to-give-advice-about-religious-issues-fewer-trust-clergy-on-personal-matters/

177 Wuthnow, R. (2022). Religion, democracy & the task of restoring trust. *Daedalus, 151*(4), 200–214. https://doi.org/10.1162/daed_a_01951

178 Burke, D. (2019, January 11). *Catholics are losing faith in clergy and church after sexual abuse scandal, Gallup survey says.* CNN. https://www.cnn.com/2019/01/11/us/catholic-gallup-survey/index.html

179 Association for Psychological Science. (2017, May 5). Group rituals can make us biased against outsiders. *ScienceDaily.* https://www.sciencedaily.com/releases/2017/05/170505121017.htm

180 Perry, S. L. (2002). American religion in the era of increasing polarization. *Annual Review of Sociology, 48*, 87–107. https://doi.org/10.1146/annurev-soc-031021-114239

181 Pew Research Center. (2019, November 15). *Americans trust both religious and nonreligious people, but most rarely discuss religion with family or friends.* Pew Research Center's Religion & Public Life Project. https://www.pewresearch.org/religion/2019/11/15/americans-trust-both-religious-and-nonreligious-people-but-most-rarely-discuss-religion-with-family-or-friends/

182 McPhetres, J., & Zuckerman, M. (2018). Religiosity predicts negative attitudes towards science and lower levels of science literacy. *PLoS ONE, 13*(11), Article e0207125. https://doi.org/10.1371/journal.pone.0207125

183 Tippins, E., Ysseldyk, R., Peneycad, C., & Anisman, H. (2023). Believing in science: Linking religious beliefs and identity with vaccination intentions and trust in science during the COVID-19 pandemic. *Public Understanding of Science, 32*(8), 1003–1020. https://doi.org/10.1177/09636625231174845

184 Luong, G., Charles, S. T., & Fingerman, K. L. (2011). Better with age: Social relationships across adulthood. *Journal of Social and Personal Relationships, 28*(1), 9–23. https://doi.org/10.1177/0265407510391362

185 Claridge, T. (2020, October 12). *Trust and Trustworthiness: An aspect of the relational dimension of social capital.* Institute for Social Capital. www.socialcapitalresearch.com/trust-and-trustworthiness/.

186 Bracht, E. M., Keng-Highberger, F. T., Avolio, B. J., & Huang, Y. (2021). Take a "selfie": Examining how leaders emerge from leader self-awareness, self-leadership, and self-efficacy. *Frontiers in Psychology, 12,* Article 635085. https://doi.org/10.3389/fpsyg.2021.635085

ACKNOWLEDGMENTS

I have many people to thank, but my family stands out for playing a tremendous role in their positive support and energy. My wife, Estelle, deserves top billing for reading the entire first draft and still encouraging me to pursue the goal of publishing. Her support and love have meant everything to me for well over the thirty years that we have been married.

Borrowing from his University of Chicago Booth School of Business background, our son, Joel, made the wise recommendation to add some type of 2x2 framework for decision-making, which I designed to help with the practical application of key insights. Daughters Sabrina and Ariel were steadfast in their positive support of the project and gave me a thumbs-up whenever there was doubt. I could not have asked for anything more from the people who mean the most to me and make me so proud.

I also want to express my deep gratitude to my brother Philip for the steady, day-to-day oversight he provides for our mother who has Alzheimer's. While family support is sometimes assumed, it merits highlighting because tasks like writing a book are only possible when support truly exists.

I owe many of the insights and stories to all the individuals whom I have had the opportunity to collaborate with, learn from, be led by, and lead. Experience is a willing teacher, yet it takes the patience and teamwork of those around you to believe in you, especially when circumstances do not always go as planned. Even reluctant employees and overmatched bosses provided great growth opportunities to test different approaches and refine my leadership expertise to be able to filter theory from reality.

Life is much bigger than a professional career and those that I play basketball with, coached in youth sports, served alongside on nonprofit boards, and shared other meaningful moments are well worthy of mentioning as having impacted my leadership tool set as well. I appreciated all those interactions and the many friendships throughout my journey.

Consistent with my beliefs and ultimate trust, I thank G-d for everything I am and do.

ABOUT THE AUTHOR

Michael Rabinowitz is a life sciences executive who has spent over thirty years driving growth and value for companies with over 100,000 employees and start-ups as small as 25 employees. He has held C-suite, consulting, and other leadership roles in strategy, marketing, sales, finance, and business development functions in the US and globally, overseeing large teams or working without a staff.

Within those roles, Michael has successfully launched billion-dollar products, turned around struggling businesses, developed innovative programs that transformed industry practice, and partnered with private and public industry leaders to advance healthcare around the world. Michael currently advises biotech and medtech CEOs in strategy and partnering as Founder and Principal of Intelluvia LLC. He has been the keynote speaker and invited guest at conferences and other events in several countries, typically focusing on leadership and business strategy. Michael also hosts a bi-weekly leadership podcast, Win Via Trust, rated in the top 10 for management podcasts in which he interviews leaders and newsmakers to share their stories and practical advice about trust.

Michael holds an MBA from The Carlson School of Management, University of Minnesota, and a BA summa cum laude from Northwestern University. He has also participated in executive healthcare programs at the Harvard Business School of Harvard University and the Wharton School of the University of Pennsylvania.

Michael is married with three children. He is highly active in the community, currently serving as vice president of the Bucks County Community College Foundation (Pennsylvania) and has been on several other charity boards. He coached youth basketball and soccer for over a decade and served in multiple roles supporting the local Boy Scouts chapter.

These professional and community roles have given Michael a broad and deep expertise in trust and leadership, which he is happy to share.